P9-CEA-649

DATE DUE

PRINTED IN U.S.A.

BirdNote

BirdNote

Chirps, Quirks, and Stories of 100 Birds from
the Popular Public Radio Show

Written by **BirdNote**

Edited by **Ellen Blackstone**

Foreword by **John W. Fitzpatrick**

Introduction by **Gordon Orians**

Illustrated by **Emily Poole**

SASQUATCH BOOKS
SEATTLE

To Chris Peterson, for her vision, leadership, and passion for birds

Printed in China
Published by Sasquatch Books

22 21 20 19 18   9 8 7 6 5 4 3 2 1

Editor: Gary Luke
Production editor: Em Gale
Design: Tony Ong
Illustrations: Emily Poole
Copyeditor: Janice Lee

Library of Congress Cataloging-in-Publication Data is available.

ISBN: 978-1-63217-169-6

Sasquatch Books
1904 Third Avenue, Suite 710
Seattle, WA 98101
(206) 467-4300
www.sasquatchbooks.com

Contents

Foreword

ONE MORNING BACK IN 2004, while working in my office overlooking Sapsucker Woods Pond, I received a phone call from Chris Peterson. At that time, Chris was executive director of Seattle Audubon, which I knew to be one of the most active and forward-thinking of the hundreds of Audubon chapters around the country. Chris had hatched a novel and ambitious idea, and was wondering if the Cornell Lab of Ornithology might be interested in playing a role. She was searching for a way to promote appreciation of birds and nature more widely than can be done through local nature centers and environmental classes. Her idea was to create a series of engaging stories about birds, to be broadcast around the country via two-minute slots. Knowing that the Cornell Lab was home to the Macaulay Library—the world's premier archive of acoustic recordings from nature—she wondered if we'd be interested in providing the bird sounds. Without hesitation, my response to Chris's question was, "Absolutely, yes!" For one thing, I remembered that the Cornell Lab itself had created a similar program back in the early 1990s, called BirdWatch (written and narrated by Bob Kantor). That show was excellent but short lived, and since becoming director of the Lab in 1995, I had wondered how our great collection of bird sounds might get back on the air. Chris's idea was a brilliant solution. Secondly, I had long appreciated the power of radio for effective storytelling. Uncluttered by visual content, good audio stories accompanied by authentic sounds have captured our attention and unleashed our human imaginations since the very first days of radio. What better way than this to open the world of birds and nature to an increasingly urbanized general public?

Birds are nature's most effective communicators to humans, and I think that this stems from their ability to stimulate both sides of our brain. Our aesthetic consciousness is drawn to their sheer beauty, their diversity, their ability to fly, and their remarkable, continent-scale migrations that mark the changing seasons. It is no wonder that artists from the earliest cave painters to the post-modernists have depicted birds in visual representations of every possible motif. So too have poets and songwriters since Homer's era embraced the spiritual power of birds, as the voices of thrushes, larks, and nightingales open our hearts to nature. Birds also appeal to our intellectual side, because they teach us how nature works. Their accessibility and diversity make them so amenable to scientific study that most modern principles in ecology, evolution, animal behavior, and natural resource management are rooted in studies of birds. Moreover, as humans increasingly change the course of the natural world, birds provide sensitive barometers for measuring the health of our natural systems.

BirdNote stories brilliantly express all these contexts, from the purely aesthetic to the technical sciences of ornithology. Tightly constructed and informative stories, interwoven with evocative natural sounds, connect us to the richly varied world of birds. I can think of no better way for the world to experience first-hand the recordings of the Macaulay Library, so it is especially grat-ifying that *BirdNote* has become such a popular radio spot and podcast. The Cornell Lab of Ornithology is privileged indeed to be closely involved with this terrific piece of media history. Our ongoing contributions to *BirdNote* productions reflect the Lab's deep commitment to outstanding partners who are dedicated to education and biodiversity conservation.

Finally, I encourage readers of this book to take note of the link provided with the list of shows, which connects to these stories on BirdNote.org. For those interested in exploring even further, all the hundreds of thousands of bird sounds archived at the Cornell Lab are available for free browsing and listening at MacaulayLibrary.org.

Long live *BirdNote*! There is no end to the astounding variety of stories yet to be told from the world of birds, and likewise no end exists to the variety of sounds of nature. So, at thirteen years and counting, I trust that this great radio program is just getting started.

—**John W. Fitzpatrick, director,**
Cornell Lab of Ornithology

Introduction

BIRDS FASCINATE US in part because, like us, they are primarily visual and vocal animals. We hear their songs and see their colorful feathers. And above all, we envy their power of flight.

Humans have been involved with birds for many thousands of years. Our remote ancestors probably valued birds and their eggs primarily as nutritious foods. But symbolic involvement with birds also began in those earlier times, as shown in prehistoric cave paintings and the presence of feathers, especially those of eagles, crows, and ravens, in ancient graves. Even Neanderthals used bird feathers or claws as personal ornaments. The antiquity of people's relationships with birds is also recorded in the myths of many cultures. Nearly all indigenous people of the North Pacific Coast of North America have raven and eagle stories. Although details of each culture's raven stories differ, certain attributes are nearly universal: the raven is always a magical creature able to take the form of a human, animal, or even inanimate object. It is a keeper of secrets, a trickster. Raven stories tell how worldly things came to be; they may also tell children how to behave.

Birds with unusual features have long attracted special interest. The Hoopoe, a bird with a long, thin beak and a strikingly crested head, turns up in the Quran, in a story about King Solomon and the queen of Sheba. Its striking appearance made the Hoopoe conspicuous. But the bird also attracted attention because it mysteriously disappeared in the autumn, only to appear again in spring. We can look to the Greeks to find some of the earliest recordings of bird migration—as far back as three thousand years ago in the writings of Homer and Aristotle. And the book of Job in the Bible, dating back to around the second millennium BC, mentions migrations of storks, swallows, and doves.

Birds have also served important utilitarian purposes. Well into the twentieth century, coal miners took canaries into the mines as an early-warning system. If dangerous gases collected in the mine, the birds, more sensitive than humans, became sick, thus alerting the miners, who could then escape or don protective respirators. Chinese fishermen still use tame cormorants to fish for them. For centuries, people have trained falcons and eagles to hunt. Homing pigeons carried valuable messages during World War I. Seafaring people have long used birds as navigational aids. Today, people of the Poluwat Atoll in the Caroline Islands navigate across vast distances between islands by dead reckoning, but when they become lost, they rely on the behavior of seabirds. A tern with a fish in its bill is certainly headed for land.

Although humans have benefited from birds in many ways for millennia, we have not always been kind to them. Many species of birds, especially those on islands, have been driven to extinction. In North America, Passenger Pigeons, numbering in the billions, completely disappeared by the early 1900s. The beautiful feathers we admire have led to devastating consequences for birds. Demand for plumes for the hat trade led to a huge decline in egrets, herons, and more. But a few people cared and stepped in to help. The National Audubon Society was formed in 1905 to protect birds in the United States and discourage the practice. Over time (and with immense public will), the demand for ornamental feathers decreased. And thanks to the resilience of birds, their populations rebounded. In the 1950s, DDT also took its toll, especially on birds of prey at the top of the food chain.

Once again, public resolve led to action, DDT was banned, and many species that were once nearly extinct in the United States are now thriving.

Today, thanks to science and technology, we're learning many new things about birds, their abilities, and their remote history. New genetic technology has surprised us by indicating that falcons are more closely related to parrots than to hawks or eagles. Using powerful computers to analyze large data sets enables us to identify the places and habitats most in need of protection so that we can establish Important Bird Areas. Tiny GPS transmitters allow us to track birds through storms and on migration. Clever experiments, combined with modern methods of analyzing brain functioning, have demonstrated that, in regard to certain tasks, crows are as intelligent as seven-year-old children.

When the wild population of California Condors was rapidly declining, heading toward extinction, biologists captured the remaining birds and transferred them to a captive breeding facility. In 1992, the US Fish and Wildlife Service began reintroducing the birds to the wild. From a low of only twenty-seven birds living in captivity, there are today more than ten times that number, living and breeding in the wild. Condors are still being poisoned when they ingest lead pellets in deer carcasses, but efforts are now under way in several states to substitute steel for lead in bullets. Thanks to concern and intervention, we can look forward to seeing condors flying in areas of the West from which they have been absent for more than a hundred years.

By telling inspiring stories about the amazing lives of birds, *BirdNote* opens a door to conservation. When people notice birds, they begin to care about them. When they care, they take steps to *protect* birds and their habitats. *BirdNote* also informs the public of the challenges birds face today, helping people understand how the needs of humans are intrinsically connected to the health of the natural world. By building widespread awareness and appreciation of birds, *BirdNote* stimulates active stewardship of nature.

The success stories of the restoration of the condor and many other birds demonstrate that even though we have at times caused great damage, we have also made great progress. There is hope. We know birds can rebound. Restoration can occur in many ways. Sometimes it means doing *something*—like teaching Whooping Cranes to follow an ultralight airplane or tracking Red Knots on migration to learn what they eat and where. But in many cases, it means doing nothing, in large ways and small—*not* cutting the juniper on a Texas Hill Country ranch, not mowing the roadside where birds are nesting, not cutting the seedheads in the garden but instead leaving them as winter bird food. When a few people care enough, the situation can be improved for birds.

BirdNote offers these stories as welcome moments of pure joy and as respite from the daily news cycle. They invite us simply to share in the delight and mystery of birds. They allow us to take solace in the memory of birdsong, find hope in the resilience of these beautiful creatures, and marvel at how they adapt to so much change and challenge in the world we share. And they seed and nourish a lifelong love of birds, empowering us to take personal steps to ensure they will be around to enrich our lives for generations to come.

**—Gordon Orians, professor emeritus of biology,
University of Washington**

The BirdNote Story

BIRDNOTE BEGAN IN 2004 as a project under the auspices of Seattle Audubon. *BirdNote* founder Chris Peterson, then executive director of Seattle Audubon, gathered a team of writers to craft compelling stories about the intriguing ways of birds. Ornithological advisers ensured scientific accuracy. A professional narrator and sound engineer gave voice to the stories. And dedicated staff, volunteers, and contractors helped form the final product. With support from benefactors, *BirdNote* was launched on air in February 2005 by KPLU-FM (now KNKX) of Seattle-Tacoma. In 2006 *BirdNote* was incorporated as an independent nonprofit under the name Tune In to Nature.org. Since then *BirdNote* has produced more than 1,500 shows and podcasts, as well as five videos—and counting.

The mission of *BirdNote* is to tell stories that connect listeners with the joy and wonder of nature. By sharing vivid, sound-rich stories about birds and the challenges they face, *BirdNote* inspires listeners to care about the natural world—and take steps to protect it.

The two-minute stories can be heard on air, online, and via podcast. Shows are broadcast daily to an estimated audience of 1.3 million people by more than two hundred public radio stations and other outlets across the country, as well as in Canada and the Philippines. Hundreds of thousands more listen online. Select episodes are also available via the Public Radio Exchange and embedded in *Living on Earth*, distributed by Public Radio International. The stories feature the sounds of hundreds of species of birds, most from the vast audio collection of The Macaulay Library at the Cornell Lab of Ornithology.

As an independent media producer, *BirdNote* is grateful for the airtime provided by public radio stations and for the financial support from individual donors, foundations, and corporate underwriters that make all its work possible.

For more information about *BirdNote* and for additional information about the birds featured in its stories, visit BirdNote.org.

BirdNote® | *Stories about birds,*
the environment, and more

The**Cornell**Lab
of Ornithology

Ptarmigan in Winter

WHEN WINTER TURNS the world white, some animals of the northern latitudes follow suit. Call it a seasonal change of camouflage. Best known is the ermine, a small weasel whose fur changes from brown to snow white in winter.

A few birds also change color. One such bird is the Willow Ptarmigan, a chicken-sized bird of the northern tundra known for its giddy voice. Feathered mostly brown in summer, it is utterly transfigured by an autumn molt. As snow begins to mantle its world, the newly white-feathered ptarmigan blends in superbly. When a covey of ptarmigan sit with feathers fluffed up against the cold, they resemble nothing so much as a row of oversized snowballs. Only a flick of their black tail feathers gives them away.

The ptarmigan pulls yet another winter trick. It adds dense feathering—white, of course—on both the tops and bottoms of its feet. And its claws grow longer. In winter, the ptarmigan actually quadruples the bearing surface of its feet. Which is to say, the bird grows snowshoes. Well, it's no wonder why the ptarmigan likes a good laugh.

Why Do Chickadees Come and Go?

WHETHER MOUNTAIN CHICKADEES in the Rockies (like this one), Black-caps in New England, or Chestnut-backs in the Northwest, chickadees are always worth watching at your feeder. If you've laid out a fine feast of sunflower seeds, you'll see them come in, quickly grab a seed, and fly away. If you watch carefully, you'll see one land nearby, open the seed, and eat the juicy and nutritious kernel within.

Now keep watching that chickadee. It may return immediately, but it's more likely to wait its turn. When a whole flock of chickadees moves into your yard, it looks as if they form a living conveyor belt. One chickadee after another flies to the feeder and then leaves with a seed. When they find a concentrated supply of food, such as a tray of sunflower seeds, the birds are better off taking turns than all coming in at once and squabbling over the seeds.

Nature seems to prefer order to chaos. And we have much to learn from the chickadees.

Spruce Grouse, Adapted for the Boreal Forest

IN THE BOREAL FOREST—the broad expanse of forest lying south of the Arctic—winter temperatures routinely drop to thirty degrees below zero. Birds that spend the winter in this harsh domain of spruce, pine, and other conifers rely on remarkable adaptations in order to survive.

The Spruce Grouse is one such bird. Most Spruce Grouse—rotund, chicken-like birds that weigh about a pound—remain here all year. In the snow-free summer, they forage on the ground, eating fresh greenery, insects, and berries. But in the snowy winter, the grouse live up in the trees, eating nothing but conifer needles. Lots and lots of needles.

Simple enough, right? Just keep eating. But conifer needles are both low in protein and tough to digest, because they're heavy in cellulose. To meet the energy demands of winter on needles alone, Spruce Grouse—this may seem hard to believe—*grow a bigger digestive system*. Their ventriculus (also known as a gizzard), which grinds food, may enlarge by 75 percent. And their ceca—pockets in the large intestine that process cellulose—may grow by 40 percent.

So remember the hardy Spruce Grouse each holiday season. As you stand back to admire a Christmas tree, somewhere in the northern forest a grouse is nibbling away at such a tree—one needle at a time.

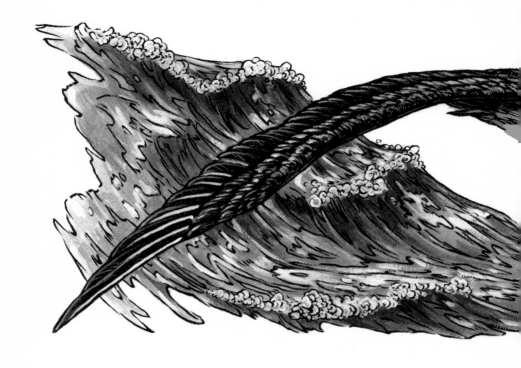

An Albatross Surfs the Wind

IMAGINE WE'RE ON a ship sailing the North Pacific—the wind must be blowing twenty-five knots. We've been watching an albatross flying in our wake for over an hour. It's an inspiring sight—this large bird with a wingspan of about seven feet is completely at home in the vastness of the open ocean. It glides up and down, back and forth, across the wake, sometimes riding up a hundred feet, then

coasting right back down near the surface. Its wings stay slightly arched, but they haven't flapped even once!

So how does this work? How can it stay with the ship without flapping its wings?

Through a marvelous feat called "dynamic soaring," the albatross uses differences in wind speed. Due to friction with the waves, the speed of the wind close to the water's surface is much slower than it is higher up. One scientist explains it this way: "An albatross, by dropping from the upper to the lower wind layer, or by rising from the lower to the upper, can gain forward speed equal to the difference in speed between the two air layers."

Northern Goshawk,
Esteemed Bird of Prey

ALL'S QUIET ON a December morning in a Northern Ontario forest. A long, narrow clearing affords a clear view of spruce and birch trees. Then, nervous yelps from a red squirrel interrupt the silence, and like a silver thunderbolt, a large bird of prey rushes by low to the ground, in rapid pursuit of a Ruffed Grouse. The grouse flaps madly, just eluding its pursuer by winging wildly into a dense thicket.

The hunter flies up to perch at the edge of the clearing. It's a Northern Goshawk, one of the most fearsome and admired of all birds of prey. Silver gray with bold white slashes above its menacing red eyes, the elegant goshawk is the largest hawk of the northern forests. Since at least medieval times, falconers have regarded the goshawk as a bird of great distinction. Attila the Hun even wore its image on his helmet.

The boreal forest is a vital part of the bird's range. Yet during lean years, when Ruffed Grouse and snowshoe hare populations dip—as happens about every ten years—the scarcity of prey brings Northern Goshawks south. It's then that we're more likely to see these beautiful and fearsome hunters.

Beak Meets Sunflower Seed

BIRDS LIKE FINCHES and cardinals love sunflower seeds, which they take into their stout, triangular beaks one after the other. In the blink of an eye, they extract the nutritious contents, and they do it so fast, it looks like a magician's sleight of hand. But if we magnify the process and slow it down, we can see how it works.

First, if we look inside a finch's beak, we see a groove that runs the length of the beak on the cutting edge of the upper half. The lower half of the beak slides into it perfectly.

When a finch—like this Cassin's Finch—plucks a sunflower seed from the feeder, it uses its tongue to maneuver the seed lengthwise into that groove. As it closes its beak, a slight back-and-forth action slices open the hull, and a small sideways movement husks the seed, while the tongue may help extract the kernel. Now it's quickly on to the next seed: maneuver, slice, husk, extract, swallow.

Chickadees lack the heavy-duty seed-slicing beak of a finch. But they still partake of countless sunflower seeds. A chickadee takes one sunflower seed at a time from the feeder, flies to a nearby perch where it holds the seed atop a branch with its foot, then hammers and chips the hull open with the tip of the bill to extract the goods.

Anna's Hummingbirds
Winter in the North

ON A CHILLY FEBRUARY morning near Seattle, with the temperature hovering below forty degrees, a bird is singing lustily. And not just any bird. It's a hummingbird! A male Anna's Hummingbird, whose throat and crown flash iridescent rose.

But what is a hummingbird doing this far north in winter? While most hummingbirds retreat south in autumn, Anna's are found in northern latitudes throughout the year. Since 1960, they've moved their year-round limit north from California to British Columbia. They're taking advantage of widely planted flowering plants and shrubs as well as hummingbird feeders.

And how do they survive the northern cold? They seem unlikely pioneers, since hummingbirds have no down feathers for insulation and a metabolism that runs so high that they would exhaust their energy reserves on a cold night.

The hummingbird's solution? Suspend that high rate of metabolism by entering a state of torpor—a sort of nightly hibernation, during which heart rate and body temperature are reduced to a bare minimum. Many hummingbirds, such as those residing in the high Andes, rely on the same strategy.

Yes, the Anna's Hummingbird has come north to stay. And its jewel-like presence at the nectar feeder adds sparkle to any winter day.

The Secretive Varied Thrush

IF YOU HEAR the eerie song of the Varied Thrush, you may be in a moist Pacific Northwest forest, in a quiet and private place. Naturalist and artist Louis Agassiz Fuertes, one of the greatest painters of birds, called the song of the Varied Thrush "as perfectly the voice of the cool, dark, peaceful solitude . . . as could be imagined."

At first glance, a Varied Thrush may appear to be a robin. Except in winter, when it gathers in loose flocks to move to lower elevations, this shy bird prefers solitude. The intricate pattern of color on its wings resembles dappled sunlight on the forest floor. And the male has a distinctive black band across his orange breast. Listen carefully and you'll hear the overtones that turn the single sound of a Varied Thrush into a delicate minor chord.

Varied Thrushes are not often heard in the urban and suburban habitats of the Puget Sound region today, because the lowland conifer forests cover less than 1 percent of their original area.

Snowy Owls Are Here

SNOWY OWLS ARE a mystery in many ways. In some years, great numbers come south from the Arctic to reside in fields, farmlands, and shorelines. In other years, we see very few. People have long wondered where they come from and why.

In the past, it was believed that population crashes of lemmings on the owls' breeding grounds caused many owls to come south. But their movements are more complex and unpredictable than that—they are affected by weather, availability of prey, and breeding success. The years that we see many owls in the south actually seem to be the result of an *abundance* of lemmings. This owl food can lead to fantastic breeding success and throngs of hungry young owls. Many may be driven southward by competition with more dominant adult owls.

Each nomadic owl is on a lifelong journey spanning continents, in search of food. Individuals have been tracked moving from Alaska to the Canadian Arctic to Russia over the course of just a couple of years. Some wander the pack ice, hundreds of miles from land, where they feed in Arctic darkness on seabirds that they snatch from the water with their hooked talons.

When one of these Arctic wanderers comes south to reside in a farmer's field, we get to glimpse a moment in a long journey that we as humans can hardly imagine.

Sanderlings' Twinkle
of Black Feet

HERE AND THERE along winter shorelines, both on the Pacific and on the Atlantic, little flocks of pale silvery shorebirds probe at the water's edge, keeping pace with each wave's ebb and flow. These small sandpipers are called Sanderlings.

Rachel Carson, whose book *Under the Sea-Wind* set a high standard for nature writing, described Sanderlings as running "with a twinkle of black feet." Carson depicted Sanderlings foraging along the beach as "keeping in the thin film at the edge of the ebbing surf ... where puffs of blown spume or sea froth rolled like thistledown."

Sanderlings also winter in the Hawaiian Islands. In the native language, they are known as *hunakai*, or "sea foam," an apt description of the sandpipers' pale winter plumage and their nimble dance with the waves.

In the warmer months, Sanderlings nest in the extreme north, most of them north of the Arctic Circle, in remote sites in Canada, Greenland, and Siberia. In winter, however, they spread out as far as any bird in the world. Their silvery flocks are sprinkled along beaches throughout the temperate and tropic zones on six of the seven continents.

Hawk of the Prairie and Tundra

THE PLAINS AND THE PRAIRIES. Wide-open spaces where the wind blows free. Where there are few hills or elevated perches. Where the Rough-legged Hawk goes hunting.

When the air is still, it's inclined to rest, but as the wind picks up, the Rough-legged Hawk takes to the sky. It defies gravity, flying upward with just enough force, hovering in midair with rapidly beating wings and lowered feet and tail. Looking for its prey of lemmings, voles, and short-tailed mice that are active during the day.

After breeding on Arctic cliffs and tundra hillsides in summer months, Rough-legged Hawks winter all across the Northern Hemisphere. Open country is their ideal territory, where the small rodents they depend on are usually so plentiful that the hawks have enough to eat. But the rodents are cyclic, with lower populations in some years, and in those winters, Rough-legs may migrate farther and be more abundant in the Lower Forty-Eight.

Why Birds Stand on One Leg

PICTURE A DUCK—say, a Mallard—standing on just one leg. It's a wonder it doesn't tip over. Long-legged herons (like this immature Black-crowned Night-Heron), as well as short-legged ducks, geese, hawks, and gulls, often roost in a peg-legged stance while keeping the other leg tucked up into their body feathers for warmth.

On the beach, look for shorebirds balanced on one leg. On rare occasions, you may see sandpipers travel short distances hopping crazily on one leg.

What is it all about? Birds have adaptations to manage heat loss. The arteries that transport blood into the legs lie in contact with the veins that return blood to the bird's heart. The warm arteries heat the cooler veins. Because the veins also cool the arteries, the bird's feet are closer to environmental temperature and thus don't lose as much heat as they would if they were at body temperature. And as for standing on one leg, do the math: a bird with its foot tucked up reduces *by half* the amount of heat lost through its unfeathered limbs.

During winter's cold, look for sparrows and juncos fluffing out their feathers to cover both legs. And for extra warmth, they tuck their beaks under their shoulder feathers, but not under their wings, as people often say.

A Crossbill's Beak
Does the Job

A STOCKY FORAGES in a conifer—it's a Red Crossbill. Crossbills travel in small flocks in search of seeds from the cones of pines, spruces, and firs. How they obtain those seeds involves a curious adaptation of their bills.

Cross your fingers, like one does for good luck. Just like your fingertips, the long tips of the crossbill's upper and lower bill don't meet but instead cross over each other.

To feed, the bird first detaches a cone from a conifer and holds that cone parallel to a branch with its feet. The bird then bites between the scales of the cone and pries them apart by opening its bill. Holding the scales apart, the bird then dislodges the seed with its tongue.

Red Crossbills search for cones in the tops of trees, climbing around using their feet and bills, much like parrots. And strangely, they'll breed in winter, if the cone crop is good enough.

The Hardy Harlequin

SOME DUCKS DON'T sound like ducks at all. Some—like the Harlequin—squeak, earning them the nickname of "sea mice."

Harlequins are unique in the duck world in other ways as well. Alone among North American waterfowl, Harlequins breed along fast-flowing rivers and streams. Quick and agile in rushing white water, they dive to the bottom of mountain streams for food.

What kind of a name is "Harlequin" for a duck? If you're lucky enough to spot one of these rare birds in winter, perhaps along a rocky shore of the Puget Sound in Washington or Penobscot Bay in Maine, you may guess the answer.

Dressed in multicolored patches, Harlequin is the jester of traditional Italian comedy. The male duck with the jester's name is just as striking, with his slate-blue feathers and vivid white, black, and chestnut markings.

The rigorous lives of Harlequins require great adaptability—moving from fresh water to salt water, from meals of caddis fly larvae to crabs and barnacles. Some, in fact, migrate by traveling directly downstream from the mountains to the ocean. Constant, however, is their unmatched ability to swim and feed in the turbulent waters where they live.

Bohemian Waxwings:
Exquisite Winter Visitors

A LIGHT DUSTING of snow whitens the hillsides along the Columbia River, a quiet backdrop to scores of apple orchards. Most of the fruit was harvested in autumn, but apples litter the ground, and a few still hang, frozen and thawed again and again.

Suddenly a flock of hundreds of birds rises from the ground beneath the apple trees, swarming in tight formation, wingtip to wingtip. The flock lifts, and the birds perch in orderly ranks in the top of a nearby poplar.

These are Bohemian Waxwings, occasional visitors during the winter, down from their nesting grounds in the boreal forests of the north. They're nomads, come in search of fruit to sustain their winter wanderings.

The Bohemian Waxwing, larger kin of the Cedar Waxwing, is exquisite, with silken plumage, a jaunty crest, a black mask, and wings daubed as if with sealing wax in red, yellow, white, and black. Add to this a tail dipped in yellow, and you have a bird that seems to have sprung from a painter's palette.

Quickly the flock is off again, swirling up the canyon to adorn the winter branches of another orchard.

Goldeneyes and Whistling Wings

ON A STILL WINTER AFTERNOON, walking the shore of Puget or Long Island Sound, you'll hear them coming low across the water. Goldeneyes, also known as "whistlers," their wings sibilant, making the sound, as Ernest Hemingway wrote, of "ripping silk." You're likely to see their piercing golden eyes and the striking black and white of the male's plumage as you board a ferry or travel by boat along the shore. Sometimes in squadrons, they dive for crustaceans and mollusks. Autumn brings both species of goldeneyes, Common and Barrow's. You'll know the male Barrow's by the half-moon of white between its brilliant yellow eye and short bill.

In spring, goldeneyes return to the boreal forests of Canada and Alaska to breed and hatch their young in the cavities of trees. And you'll have to wait until next November to hear the music of their wings again.

The Majestic Gyrfalcon, Winter's Regal Visitor

WINTER SENDS WONDROUS BIRDS down from the Arctic. Unrivaled among these visitors is the majestic Gyrfalcon. Gyrfalcons are among the largest falcons in the world, with the female—the larger of the sexes—outranking even a Red-tailed Hawk in size.

With a name derived from an Old Norse word for "spear," the Gyrfalcon was a medieval falconer's prize, reserved for royalty. Kublai Khan, it is said, kept two hundred.

When hunting, the Gyrfalcon flies swiftly and low, just above the ground, hugging contours to conceal its attack. A Gyrfalcon is capable of overtaking even the fastest waterfowl, some of which can fly sixty miles an hour.

On its summer range on the tundra, the falcon feeds mostly on ptarmigan. But in winter, it is opportunistic, chasing down shore-birds, ducks, partridges, and even small rodents. By December, a small number of Gyrfalcons have flown south to the northern states, where they will spend the winter in areas of open expanse, such as farmlands or coastal areas. Perhaps the prince of falcons awaits you out there.

Leaping Sandhill Cranes

IN THE ROSY GLOW of a sunrise on a southwestern marsh, a pair of Sandhill Cranes calls in unison. With a graceful leap, wings outstretched, the two cranes welcome the last days of February.

The stately cranes are courting, renewing an annual dance they perform in earnest as the days lengthen into spring. The dance begins with a downward bow, the cranes' long, slender bills nearly touching the ground. Then, like enormous marionettes pulled deftly upward, the cranes leap several feet off the ground, wings outstretched. Bowing and leaping, raising and lowering their wings, the cranes dance on as the sun rises.

Sandhill Crane pairs remain together for life, and their spirited dance plays an essential role in reaffirming this bond. The cranes' exquisite dance complements beautifully their rich, rolling calls— one of nature's most memorable anthems. The elegant Sandhills will leap and dance a few days more before migrating north to nest.

Woodpeckers ♥ Ants

AN EXPERT WOOD-CARVER is hard at work. A sixteen-inch Pileated Woodpecker is hammering its massive chisel of a bill against a cedar trunk, making large, rectangular incisions—some nearly a foot long.

This carpenter seeks out another. Within the trunk swarm many thousands of carpenter ants. The half-inch-long insects have themselves excavated a nesting colony in the heart of the living tree.

The woodpecker's sticky tongue reaches five inches beyond the tip of its bill into the trunk, lapping up hundreds of ants. They may make up more than half of the Pileated's entire food intake.

Woodpeckers as a group eat far more ants than do most birds, swallowing them whole. Many other vertebrates studiously avoid ants because of their stings or noxious chemical deterrents, like formic acid. Another member of the woodpecker family, the Northern Flicker, is known to have ingested over five thousand ants in one sitting.

While the Pileated Woodpecker and Northern Flicker also eat a variety of other insects and berries, they always love to have a good supply of ants.

Ruffed Grouse Drumming in the Forest

IMAGINE THIS: you're at the edge of a forest dominated by aspen. And you're hearing this accelerating thumping sound. What's going on in there? Is somebody starting up an engine?

It's a male Ruffed Grouse performing his drumming display. He's the size and shape of a large rusty-brown chicken, and he's standing on a resonant fallen log in the shelter of a brushy thicket. He's thumping the air with his wings. He raises them and—cupping them forward—beats the air, slowly at first, then faster and faster, creating a reverberating drumroll. Drumming announces a male's territory and his desire for a mate.

The Ruffed Grouse takes its name from the male's long neck feathers, which—in display to the female—flex outward to form a thick ruff. It's typically a shy denizen of the forest. But in spring, the Ruffed Grouse is a star percussionist in nature's symphony.

The Aquatic American Dipper

A BRILLIANT SONG rings out over a rapidly rushing western stream. It belongs to an American Dipper, a songbird the color of wet gray stones. The dipper looks like a large, chubby wren—or perhaps a gray robin with a very short tail. Standing atop a large stone, it bobs up and down on its long legs—"dipping"—hence the name.

But watch this nondescript bird a moment: it steps off a small boulder right into the torrent and begins to peer underwater. Then, raising its head, it blinks, showing white-feathered eyelids. Soon it is swimming in the stream, paddling with its feet. Suddenly it dives—and holds its place underwater with its short, strong wings—against a coursing flow that would knock a person right over. Just as briskly, it pops back up on a small boulder and, using its bill, begins to hammer the casing of a tasty caddis fly larva it just picked off the stream bottom.

What the American Dipper might lack in bright color it more than surpasses with amazing aquatic abilities. It's the only aquatic songbird in North America.

Storks and Babies

STORKS AND BABIES have been linked for centuries. But how did that old legend that storks bring babies get started? Researchers suggest that the legend goes back to pagan times, when civilizations were keen to have high birth rates. It probably began in what is now Northern Germany.

The legend concerns the White Stork, a large, stately bird with black wings, red legs, and a red bill. These birds breed in Europe but migrate far to the south to winter in tropical Africa. The link between storks and babies was forged by the birds' return in spring, a time when many babies were born, just about nine months after midsummer.

The association with babies has been propitious for the storks. People encouraged the birds to build their large stick nests on roofs and chimneys. Even today, many people associate storks with good luck and look forward to their return each spring.

Pigeon Babies Do Exist

EVERY SPRING, DOWN-COVERED Mallard ducklings follow their mother across a pond. Goslings graze alongside their Canada Geese parents in waterfront parks. Baby chickens peck the ground soon after hatching. But why do we never see baby pigeons?

Some baby birds—like those ducks, geese, and chickens—leave their nest shortly after hatching and do a lot of growing up while following their parents around. Others, like pigeons, stay in the nest and depend on their parents to feed and protect them well into their youth.

When young Rock Pigeons finally leave the nest, they are full-size, with adult feathers, and they look like their parents. So unless you look carefully under a city bridge, you aren't likely to ever see a baby pigeon.

It's easy to imagine, when hearing the adults' soft cooing sounds, why baby pigeons would rather stay in the nest. They wait to fledge until they are nearly independent and the task of getting on with life is a bit easier.

Spider Silk and Bird Nests

A SPIDER'S WEB is an intricate piece of precision engineering. And the spider silk it is constructed with is amazing. Made from large proteins, it is sticky, stretchy, and tough. So it's no surprise that many small birds make a point of collecting strands of spider silk to use in nest construction—birds like hummingbirds, kinglets, gnatcatchers, and some vireos.

Golden-crowned Kinglets, which are among the smallest of songbirds, build a tiny square nest. They often use strands of spider silk to suspend the structure from adjoining twigs, like a tiny hammock.

When a female Ruby-throated Hummingbird is building her nest, she collects the spider silk she needs by sticking it all over her beak and breast. When she reaches the nest site, she'll press and stretch the silk onto the other materials—such as lichen and moss—creating a tough, tiny cup. Spider silk not only acts as a glue, holding the other bits together, but it is flexible enough to accommodate the growing bodies of nestlings. And it is resilient enough to withstand all the bustle of raising those hungry babies.

Where we might reach for duct tape, birds turn to spider silk.

Bushtit, a Very Tiny Songbird

ONLY A FEW SONGBIRDS anywhere in the world are as small as Bushtits. Weighing in at 5.3 grams—that's about equal to four paper clips—they are smaller than many hummingbirds. Take a close look at a Bushtit, and you'll marvel at how tiny it is.

But Bushtits take full advantage of their diminutive size. While larger insect-eaters forage on the upper surfaces of leaves and twigs, Bushtits hang beneath them. That gives them exclusive access to all the tiny insects and spiders protecting themselves from the rain and hiding out of sight of other birds. Watch a foraging flock of Bushtits and you'll have to smile. A shrub or small tree may be full of little brown long-tailed birds hanging upside down like Christmas-tree ornaments.

After they finish nesting, Bushtits go about in flocks of thirty or more. One bird after another flies from bush to bush, like a troop passing in review. Their quiet calls help them keep track of one another. Where they live in suburbia, a flock of thirty Bushtits can do a great job of ridding a garden of harmful aphids and scale insects. Good things do come in small packages!

Acorn Woodpeckers Create Granaries, One Acorn at a Time

A LARGE, DARK WOODPECKER clings to the side of a tree. Its face is almost clown-like, boldly patterned in black and cream, with a red crown. And it's holding something in its bill. Eyeing the tree with care, the woodpecker wedges the object into a shallow hole. A closer look reveals thousands of these small pockets in the bark, most neatly filled with acorns.

The bird is an Acorn Woodpecker, and it is found in parts of the western United States. It chips out these little recesses to fit the acorns it will harvest throughout the fall. A family of Acorn Woodpeckers may use this storage tree, or granary, for generations. Some of them hold as many as fifty thousand acorns, which the woodpeckers rely on when insect prey and other foods are hard to come by. But if trees with thick bark are in short supply, utility poles, fence posts, or the sides of barns will serve the same purpose.

So does the Acorn Woodpecker just kick back and munch acorns all winter? Not a chance. Because in the weeks after a fresh acorn is lodged in a hole, it dries and shrinks. Meaning Acorn Woodpeckers spend much of the winter shuttling them from one hole to another, finding just the right fit.

Eurasian Collared-Doves' Sense of Direction

THE EURASIAN COLLARED-DOVE population is rapidly increasing across the United States and southern Canada. But not in every direction. This sandy-pink bird with the neat black neckband is a native of Asia. Several captive birds were released in the Bahamas in the 1960s, when their enclosures were destroyed in a storm. They made it to the Florida mainland a few years later and have been spreading ever since, but generally in a west-northwest direction.

Now collared-doves are more common on the coasts of British Columbia than they are in some areas closer to where they started out. Yet no one knows why they keep so strictly to this northwest bearing. In Europe too they've been pushing northwest, starting in the Balkans, reaching Britain by the 1950s, and even moving on to the Faroe Islands and Iceland. All this before they managed to make the much shorter step from the Balkans south into Africa.

Now, true to their inner compass, collared-doves appear poised to conquer another territory: Alaska. From their starting point of the Bahamas, that's about as far northwest as it gets.

Which Jay Was That?

A RAUCOUS CRY—what bird made that sound? It's a jay—and it's blue. But this is a Steller's Jay, not a true Blue Jay with a capital *B*. The bona fide Blue Jay is primarily a bird of the East, or east of the Rocky Mountains at least. Of the many jays in the United States, these are the only two that sport crests.

These jays have similar personalities. Both are raucous and have a bit of a reputation for being "bad boys." Nineteenth-century zoologist, Thomas Nuttall, wrote of the Steller's Jay that "they are as watchful as dogs" and that "they . . . come round, follow, peep at and scold [you]." And Mark Twain said the Blue Jay "hasn't any more principle than an ex-congressman, and he will steal, deceive, and betray four times out of five."

Like their larger cousins, the crows and ravens and magpies, Blue Jays and Steller's Jays are intelligent opportunists. They've adapted to living near people, and they are the masters of the back-yard birdfeeder. Both have good memories. And they are not shy about asking for a handout.

What in the World
Is a Hoopoe?

A PATTERN OF THREE soft and modest hoots signals a bird so distinctive, so fabled, that it is hard to know where to begin its story. Let's start with the bird's name, Hoopoe—or Hoopo—(pronounced HOO-poo), modeled on its song. Its scientific name too comes from those mellow hoots: *Upupa epops.*

The Hoopoe is the only extant member of a unique family of birds: Upupidae. And it's a crazy-looking bird: jay sized, with a long bill like a sandpiper's. The Hoopoe's head and breast are buffy pink, with a crest it can raise like a Native American headdress. It flies on rounded, boldly zebra-striped wings, fluttering unevenly like a giant butterfly.

Found through much of the Old World, it's a bird so peculiar that it has caught the eye of humans for eons. The Hoopoe figures in mythologies of Arabic, Greek, Persian, Egyptian, and other cultures. But the bird's fame hasn't gone to its head. In all its oddity, the humble Hoopoe carries on with a minimum of fuss, nesting in tree cavities in Europe and Asia and migrating to the warmth of Africa in winter.

Red-winged Blackbird Harem

WELCOME TO SPRING! Step into a lively cattail marsh and surround yourself with the sound of glossy black birds with bright-red shoulder patches. These are male Red-winged Blackbirds.

The male brandishes his red epaulets to warn other male Red-winged Blackbirds away from his patch of cattails. At the same time, he sings to lure females into his marshy territory—*many* females, in fact.

While birds of most other species pair up and form twosomes during the spring breeding season, the Red-winged Blackbird has a different strategy. One male will claim a territory and attract up to a dozen females to form a harem.

These females look nothing like the males. They're smaller, with mottled brown backs and heavily streaked bellies. Each female weaves an intricate nest, often suspended over the water. Scientists examined one nest that contained 142 cattail leaves, 705 pieces of grass, and 34 strips of willow bark.

And while she's building that amazing nest, the male is busy fending off other males and courting more females for his harem.

Earthworm, a Superfood
in Cold Storage

A ROBIN TUGGING an earthworm from the ground in spring or summer is the quintessential image of a backyard bird. But as fall gives way to winter, many earthworms in cooler parts of the country retreat deeper into the soil, to warmer realms beyond the robin's reach. At this time of year, these normally solitary birds flock together in an adaptive strategy that makes it easier to find fruits and berries on widely scattered trees and shrubs.

The ground begins to warm in spring, though. The robins start to notice slight movements in the soil from the worms' burrows—and once again seek out these nutritious invertebrates. Everyday earthworms are higher in protein content than either beef or chicken; you'd have to eat around a pound of soybeans to equal the protein in just three ounces of earthworms. And they're high in calcium and easy to catch, compared to an agile cricket or a butterfly.

Put that all together, and you have pretty much a superfood for birds—and youngsters in particular. The worms hide deep in the soil throughout the winter, until a springtime date with destiny—and the beak of an American Robin.

Ravens and Crows—
Who's Who?

SO YOU'RE WALKING down the street, minding your own business. And a trash can has been tipped over. Eagerly picking through the riches strewn across the sidewalk are several black birds. They're crows. Or ravens. No, definitely crows—maybe.

How can you tell the difference? Well, first off, crows give a cawing sound. But ravens are croakers.

And while Common Ravens and American Crows look quite similar, there are a few key distinguishing features that can help you tell one from the other.

Ravens are larger, the size of a Red-tailed Hawk. And they often travel in pairs, while crows are seen in larger groups. Also, watch the bird's tail as it flies overhead. The crow's tail feathers are basically all the same length, so when the bird spreads its tail, it opens like a fan. But ravens have longer feathers in the middle of their tails, so their tails appear wedge shaped when open.

But the bill is the really easy way to tell. The raven has a chunky, gray-black, menacing-looking beak that pretty much says, "Yeah, that's right. I'm a raven. So?" The crow's bill, on the other hand, is somewhat more modest. And if you see a black bird picking through the trash, it's most likely a crow. Ravens prefer the woodlands and open spaces. They're a bit more on the wild side.

Double-crested Cormorant

DEEP, GUTTURAL SOUNDS are coming from a nesting colony of Double-crested Cormorants—large black waterbirds with short legs and long necks. If you look closely, you can see the bird's double crest—its two long, gloriously feathered eyebrows. When not nesting, Double-crested Cormorants are a common sight near fresh and salt water. They often sit upright on a rock or piling, holding their wings out to the sides, resembling a black Celtic cross. During courtship, they may wave their outstretched wings.

Why do they have such a limited and guttural vocal range when many birds create glorious songs? It has to do with the number of muscles a bird can use to govern its vocal organ, the syrinx. The more muscles they have, the more elaborate the sound. Many songbirds have five to seven sets of these muscles. The cormorant has only one.

The Ballet of the Grebes

WHEN WESTERN GREBES decide it's time to mate, it's as if they know they have an audience for the performance they're about to give. On the still waters of an alkaline lake, they call loudly and approach one another. Each bird gracefully curves, then straightens, its long neck.

They then face each other, necks on the water's surface, their bills flipping up drops of water. If attraction prevails, they rush together and off they go across the water, running side by side on the surface. Standing straight up with necks held high and feet churning like propellers, they no longer look much like grebes—more like participants in Tchaikovsky's ballet *Swan Lake*.

After their lengthy pas de deux, with wings extended like parallel sails, they plunge below the surface. What follows is the "weed ceremony," in which each bird dives to pick up a beakful of soft vegetation. The grebes then stand up in the water, face one another, press tightly together, drop the plants, and preen. The whole courtship sequence may begin again at any time, building in intensity as spring progresses and the pair makes ready to start a new generation.

American Kestrel

THE AMERICAN KESTREL is small, numerous, and widespread. Watch for one of these North American falcons perched on a utility wire, bobbing its tail.

Like others of the falcon family, the American Kestrel is built for speed, with long, pointed wings, often bent back at the tip. If a suitable perch isn't available, American Kestrels will hover above an open field. Facing into the wind, they flap their wings and use their tails to hold their positions. From above, kestrels watch for insects, small mammals, and reptiles, which they overtake and capture. Don't be fooled by their small size (equal to that of a robin)—these are fierce hunters. Using their notched beaks, kestrels quickly subdue their prey by severing the spinal cord at the neck.

The lack of suitable nesting cavities limits kestrel populations in some areas. And this has led people to install wooden nest boxes. Many states now have programs to place kestrel nest boxes along interstate highways. On I-35 in Iowa, there's a kestrel box nearly every mile, from the border of Minnesota to that of Missouri. The kestrels readily adapt to these boxes and return each spring to set up house.

Small Birds Mob Big Ones

HAVE YOU EVER WATCHED crows dive-bombing a hawk or an eagle? Several crows will gang up and pester a larger bird into leaving their breeding territory. Perhaps you've seen starlings or blackbirds do the same to crows.

When smaller birds join forces to ward off larger birds, it's called "mobbing." This behavior—like calling family members for help—is used by many bird species. The best time to observe mobbing is spring and early summer, when breeding birds are trying to protect their nests and young.

Barn Swallows, which nest near humans, are a good example. If a few swallows perceive a threat—maybe this Northern Pygmy-Owl—to their nesting territory, they sound the alarm. Half a dozen neighboring swallows will arrive almost immediately to help scare away the intruder, be it a house cat slinking into the garden or you venturing too close.

If you hear a ruckus and spot several crows circling and swooping toward a tall conifer, it's a good bet that there's a raptor tucked in the tree, a hawk perhaps, or an owl.

These birds know that there's strength in numbers, and they've learned to join forces to protect themselves.

Green Heron

OF ALL THE HERONS you might see, the most likely is the tall, elegant Great Blue Heron. But that stately bird has a much smaller and more secretive relative—the Green Heron. This chunky, short-legged heron is about one-third the size of its larger cousin.

The Green Heron forages on the banks of small bodies of fresh water with trees and shrubs nearby. Relying on its forest-green and chestnut-colored plumage for camouflage, it perches motionless. With its body horizontal and stretched forward, the heron waits for small fish to come close.

Now here's the fascinating part. This heron sometimes uses bait to attract fish. It breaks twigs into pieces small enough to make convincing lures. It cleverly drops one of these tiny twigs—or maybe a feather or a live insect—on the water's surface. Then it hunkers down and waits for unsuspecting prey to venture within reach of its sharp bill.

The Great Blue Heron may be easier to see, but also keep an eye out for the small—and clever—Green Heron.

How the Cactus Wren Builds Its Nest

IN LATE APRIL in the Arizona desert, it's already over ninety degrees by eleven in the morning. And the mercury is still rising. A Cactus Wren sings, perched atop a many-lobed cactus. Then it hops down to its nest, which is tucked among the spiny lobes of the prickly pear.

In a desert realm where it's hot enough to fry an egg on a flat rock, how can the delicate nestlings of a Cactus Wren survive? Well, Cactus Wrens, which may nest several times between March and September, carefully orient their nests in tune with the season. Their bulky twig structures, shaped roughly like footballs, have a side entrance. That tubular entrance curves toward the inner chamber.

When building a nest for the hot months, the wren positions the opening so that it will receive the afternoon breeze. This circulates cooling air through the chamber and over the chicks. By contrast, a Cactus Wren building a nest in early March orients the entrance away from the cold winds of that season, keeping the chicks snug and warm.

The Little Red Spot
on a Gull's Bill

YOU MAY HAVE NOTICED—on a trip to the shore or at a waterfront restaurant where gulls gather—that many gulls have a bright-red spot near the tip of their otherwise yellow bills. Behind that red spot lies a considerable tale.

In the mid-twentieth century, Dutch scientist Niko Tinbergen studied nesting Herring Gulls. He noticed that newly hatched gull chicks were fed by their parents only after they pecked at the adults' bills. Tinbergen devised experiments that varied the shape and coloration of the adult's bill. He concluded that the red spot on the adult gull's bill was a crucial visual cue in a chick's demands to be fed and was thus essential to its survival.

Tinbergen also made the case that the chick's attraction to the red spot on the bill was instinctive. This conclusion came at a time when there was furious debate among experts about whether such behavior was learned or innate.

Turns out that it's more complicated than that. But Tinbergen's gull research helped lay the groundwork for the science of animal behavior and earned him a Nobel Prize in 1973. And it all started with that little red spot.

The Superbly
Adapted Osprey

TO THE UNTRAINED EYE, the Osprey looks just like a bird of prey should. Talons, hooked beak, vivid yellow eyes. But it also has some characteristics that make it truly unique among raptors. Especially when catching fish.

Like most raptors, it has four long toes—three in front and one in back. As the bird reaches for a fish, its outer front toe swivels to the rear, giving it two grasping talons in the front and in the back. And those toes are lined with short, stiff spikes for extra grip. The Osprey's nostrils shut tight as it hits the water. Then as it ascends, it shakes itself off, shedding water easily thanks to its oily feathers. In fact, it's the only raptor that has this oily plumage. Its long, slender, arched wings help it get clear of the water too as it takes flight with the fish's head facing the front—the most aerodynamically efficient position.

This Osprey we see today—just one species worldwide—has changed little since tens of millions of years ago, when its ancestors diverged onto a unique evolutionary track, distinct from eagles and hawks, suggesting that over this period, it has remained particularly well suited to its environment, thanks to these adaptations.

Why the Black Skimmer Skims

IF YOU ARE FORTUNATE enough to hear a Black Skimmer in flight, you might think you're hearing a dog barking in the distance. An unusual sound for a bird, yes. And this striking black-and-white bird with a red bill and red feet has a most unusual way of feeding too. It flies low along the surface of the water with its beak open. The bird's long and narrow lower mandible angles down into the water.

When it strikes a small fish, the shorter, curved upper bill snaps shut. The skimmer rises into the air and swallows its prey or takes it back to its young. If the bill hits an immovable object on the water's surface, the bird pivots upward, and the lower mandible slides right over it, amusing to the onlooker if not to the skimmer. As skimmers feed by touch, they continue foraging at night, when they are less visible to their prey.

Closely related to terns, skimmers nest on sand islands in closely packed colonies. They depend on undisturbed islands and abundant small fish, both characteristic of the coastal lagoons of the Atlantic Flyway.

The Marsh Wren's Many Nests

IMAGINE A MAN, in wooing a mate, needing to frame and cover four, ten, or even fifteen houses before his intended chooses the one she likes and he wins her over. That is precisely what the male Marsh Wren must do!

Tiny Marsh Wrens live in wetlands, usually within cattails, reeds, or bulrushes. After choosing his territory, the male weaves several dome-shaped shells, lashing together cattails, grasses, or reeds. These are called courting nests. Then, sitting high atop a perch in the marsh, he sings his sewing machine–like song, inviting a female to select a nest in his territory.

Once the female has chosen one of his shells, she lines it with cattail down, feathers, leaves, or grass and lays her eggs. Sometimes a second female chooses a nest on the opposite end of his territory. Attracting mates and confusing predators make all the male's work worthwhile.

Downy Woodpecker, Far and Wide

COAST TO COAST, border to border, forest to feeder, the Downy Woodpecker goes about its business in forty-nine states. It turns up everywhere there are trees, except Hawaii and the dry deserts of the Southwest.

The Downy is the smallest woodpecker in the United States. It might have been named by comparing it to its larger cousin, the Hairy Woodpecker, which looks quite similar. Where the Downy has soft, fluffy feathers, especially at the back of its head, the Hairy's feathers look stiff and bristly.

The flash of red on the woodpecker's head brings a bit of cheer to your winter feeder. It's the male that has the red; the female sports only black and white feathers. And there's another difference: the female searches for insects and other tasty tidbits on large limbs and the trunk of a tree, while the male works farther out, on smaller branches.

Add a suet cake to your backyard bird banquet, and you'll probably bring the Downy Woodpecker right up close.

Tree Swallows and Feathers,
an Aerial Ballet

TREE SWALLOWS GLISTEN in the June sunlight as they swoop and glide, their arcs interlacing in the air. Agile, elegant masters of flight, the swallows gather near their nest boxes, clustered on posts at the edge of a marsh.

A white feather flutters down among them. One swallow snatches the feather in its bill and flies upward as another swallow gives chase. After a moment, the lead bird lets loose the feather, which drifts lazily until the second bird swoops in to catch it in midair. The aerial ballet swirls on for minutes as other swallows join in the feather chase.

Are the swallows just playing, or are they competing for these feathers? Loose feathers are an important resource for Tree Swallows. They line their nests thickly with them, a feather bed for nestlings. Continuing research suggests that as Tree Swallows build their nests, it is the females that collect the feathers. Their aerial dance may well be a competition for nest-lining material.

And the males in the feather chase? Maybe they're just playing along.

Blakiston's Fish Owl

A SERIES OF DISTINCTIVE low hoots signals the presence of a sumo wrestler of a bird. It's Blakiston's Fish Owl—"Blakiston's" because its existence was recorded by the English naturalist Thomas Blakiston, and "Fish Owl" because it hunts fish. Standing at the edge of a stream, sometimes in the shallows, it watches intently, eyes fixed on the water. Then, with a sudden jump forward, wings upraised, it plunges its talons into a fish and pulls it onto the bank—sometimes a fish as large as a salmon.

This massive bird is the largest owl in the world. Tawny brown, a female Blakiston's Fish Owl is the larger of the sexes and may stand twenty-eight inches tall, weighing in at over ten pounds. That's the same weight as a Bald Eagle. Compared with the Great Horned Owl, the Blakiston's is six inches taller and nearly three times as heavy. No other owl approaches its prodigious girth.

But the Blakiston's Fish Owl is endangered. It is found only in wooded areas in the east of Japan's second-largest island, Hokkaido, and in small areas in nearby Russia and China. Future preservation of forest and river habitats in these regions will be crucial to the survival of this one-of-a-kind owl.

California Quail, Up and Running

IF YOU HEAR A BIRD that seems to be saying "chi-CA-go, chi-CA-go," don't be misled—that small groundbird, the California Quail, is strictly a bird of the Far West. The California Quail's gray- and rust-colored body is beautifully adorned. And the most distinctive characteristic of this quail is a forward-facing black topknot that juts out from the bird's forehead like a small flag.

Although quail can fly short distances, they spend most of their time on the ground, foraging for food. When they're threatened, they scurry into thick brush.

Quail build their well-concealed nests, which can hold one to twenty-four eggs, right on the ground. Twenty-four? Yes, the large clutches may include eggs from more than one female. Immediately after hatching, the chicks follow their parents around, scratching for food. Two or more quail families may join together to form a covey of quail. With such a large extended family, it's not surprising when a male California Quail hops up on a stump to gather the covey together with his rallying call, "chi-CA-go, chi-CA-go."

Clever Nuthatches

HAVE YOU NOTICED a sleek, stub-tailed bird pecking its way down a tree trunk? It's probably a nuthatch. It might remind you of a tiny woodpecker, but woodpeckers travel up the trunk, leaning on their tails.

Where did this bird get a name like "nuthatch"? Perhaps because this tiny songbird tucks insects, nuts, and seeds under bark or in crevices of trees. Then it hacks the tidbits apart with repetitive strikes of its beak, as if it's using a hatchet. Of the four nuthatch species living in the United States, the most common are the Red-breasted Nuthatch and the White-breasted Nuthatch. The nuthatch's insistent call matches its aggressiveness. These tough little guys will challenge birds larger than themselves for food and territory. Birds gathered around a feeder give way when a nuthatch is around.

And that business of working its way down a tree trunk? It's a clever move, because the nuthatch can spot—and eat—all the tasty morsels missed by the rest of the birds working their way up the tree.

King Penguins' Kazoo Band

WHEN IT'S STILL WINTER in many parts of North America, it's summer in Antarctica. And the birds are singing—at least the penguins are. A pair of King Penguins stands face to face. They tilt their heads back, point their long bills skyward, and trumpet in unison.

Second largest of all penguins, King Penguins stand nearly three feet tall. They are surprisingly colorful too with a bright oval of lustrous orange yellow adorning the back half of their dark heads.

Some King Penguins form breeding colonies that number in the tens of thousands. And when many pairs tip their heads back and sing, it sounds like the world's largest kazoo band.

Altogether, more than two million King Penguins nest on islands in the Southern Ocean, the sea that surrounds Antarctica. Their breeding cycle ranks among the longest of all birds. From the time the female lays her single egg in late spring, it will take about fourteen months before that chick is ready to fend for itself the following summer—we hope with a loud send-off from the immense kazoo band.

Anting: An Avian Spa Treatment?

ON A WARM, SUNNY DAY, an American Robin sits on the ground, its wings outstretched and its tail splayed behind. Look closely and you might see that the robin is sitting astride an anthill and that ants are swarming over its body! Occasionally the robin even takes an ant in its bill and wipes the ant against the underside of its wings—a kind of avian spa treatment.

This behavior, first recorded by John James Audubon in the 1830s, is known as "anting." Although observed infrequently, anting has been recorded among more than 250 species of birds. The purpose of anting remains something of a mystery, although most experts agree it has to do with transferring the ants' secretions—particularly formic acid—to the bird's body. It's likely that the ants' formic acid helps control feather mites and other parasites.

Lacking ants, some birds have been seen using citrus fruits, mothballs, and even glowing embers to achieve the effects of formic acid. One clever bird, a rook—the British cousin of the American Crow—even learned to strike a match, then touch the hot tip to its underwing.

Ruby-throated Hummingbirds Have Arrived

IT'S LATE APRIL in the Northeast. You've just stepped out for a breath of spring air and—hey, what was that? A tiny bird just whizzed by like a bullet. There it is, over by those scarlet flowers, hovering—it's a hummingbird. It must be a Ruby-throated Hummingbird, the only hummingbird that nests in the eastern states. No wonder it buzzed by you—you're wearing a red baseball cap! It must have thought you were a flower.

Most Ruby-throated Hummingbirds spend the winter in Central America. By March, some males are already returning to the southeastern United States. But it's well into April before they reach the northern states. Female hummingbirds arrive a couple weeks later, after the males have staked out breeding territories. Males greet females with a remarkable aerial performance, flying back and forth in a perfect arc, like a pendulum suspended on an invisible wire, with buzzing wings and cricket-like chirps.

So fill up the hummingbird feeder, put on a red hat or jacket, and listen for a Ruby-throat coming your way.

The Baltimore Oriole, a Blackbird with an Aristocratic Name

WHEN YOU HEAR the word "blackbird," what sort of bird do you picture? Maybe the familiar Red-winged Blackbird that sings in the marsh? Well, not all blackbirds are mostly black. One is orange and even has an aristocratic name: the Baltimore Oriole. This gorgeous golden-orange and black bird took its name from Sir George Calvert, First Lord Baltimore. His coat of arms carried a gold-and-black design.

Baltimore Orioles eat insects and fruit, but they're fussy. They go mostly for vividly colored fruit. For nesting material, on the other hand, bland is better. The female—who does all the architectural work—bypasses colorful threads and fibers and instead chooses dull colors. She's a much drabber orange and blends in with the background while incubating her eggs.

In spring and summer, you may see these orioles in the Midwest and eastern United States, lighting up the leafy trees where they nest.

You can cater to the particular taste of these beautiful birds. If you're lucky enough to live near Baltimore Orioles, entice them to your feeder with half an orange or some grape jelly!

House Sparrow Pool Party

LIKE PRETEENS AT a swimming pool, House Sparrows chatter as they splash in a birdbath. Pudgy, social, chatty, and ubiquitous, the House Sparrow has adapted to living in cities, suburbs, and rural areas. Considered by some just another "little brown bird," a closer look reveals more: the male House Sparrow's head is decorated with chestnut and gray, and he sports a black bib.

Like most birds, these sparrows enjoy a daily bath. If you set out a birdbath, you can watch them lower their heads and shimmy down into the water, wings slightly spread. Then they pop out and shake like a dog, water droplets flying.

If you've ever watched a bird bathing in a puddle, you know that birds like very shallow water; an inch or two is plenty. Be sure your birdbath has a flat rim or rocks for the birds to perch on to shake themselves dry.

If you aren't interested in setting out bird feeders, installing a birdbath can be an entertaining alternative. Chattering, gregarious House Sparrows may be the first to arrive.

The Amazing,
Head-Turning Owl

SOMETIMES, OWLS STRIKE us as downright spooky. The spine-tingling call of an Eastern Screech-Owl is a case in point. Equally eerie is an owl's ability to seemingly rotate its head in a complete circle. Are spectral forces at work here, enabling an owl to spin its head 360 degrees? Or do its neck feathers hide some anatomical secret?

Well, an owl's apparent head rotation is part illusion, part structural design. To begin with, because an owl's large eyes are fixed in their sockets, it must rotate its neck to look around.

And an owl will frequently perch with its head turned, looking over its shoulder to prevent predators from sneaking up behind. Hearing a noise from an unseen source, the owl rotates its head to the front and then around to the opposite shoulder in one quick, smooth movement, in what appears to be a full circle. Uncanny.

The actual rotation is about 270 degrees. With fourteen neck vertebrae—that's twice as many as you have—an owl can turn its head ninety degrees farther than you can. Even without any occult forces at work, this is a marvelous anatomical feat.

A Chorus Line of Bonaparte's Gulls

THE TIDE IS PARTWAY OUT. Bonaparte's Gulls, one of North America's smallest, have formed a chorus line at the water's edge. Side by side, in half an inch of water, they're stomping their feet as fast as they can. This stirs up an abundance of tiny marine invertebrates, including a smorgasbord of shrimp.

Is this a learned behavior, or are the gulls born knowing how to forage cooperatively? Most likely, it's innate, but no one knows for certain.

The Bonaparte's Gulls have returned from the boreal forest of the North, where they nest in trees. Trees? Yes, they're the only gull that regularly does that. Now, as they migrate south through the Mississippi Flyway and along both coasts, they're amassing in large flocks.

In summer, the head of the adult is still black—like a vanilla ice cream cone that's been dipped in very dark chocolate. But soon it will begin a gradual transition back to the white head of winter.

This is one gull you're never going to see in a garbage dump. Bonaparte's Gulls find food in several ways but not by picking through trash. Why should they, when they have such a nutritional dance routine?

Lewis's Woodpecker
and Pine Forests

THE LEWIS'S WOODPECKER'S glossy dark-green back, red face, and pink belly make it look as if it belongs in a tropical forest. But this species is, in fact, an icon of the American West. A temperate migrant, this bird breeds across the western states in mature ponderosa pine forests and then moves south in winter.

A century of logging and fire control has taken its toll on these mature pine forests, the preferred nest site for the Lewis's Woodpecker. It takes a long time for a ponderosa pine to grow large enough for the woodpecker to carve out a nest cavity.

As nest holes have become scarcer, so have many other species that rely on them. For example, the tiny Flammulated Owl has also declined. The moths that make up the owl's diet are absent during northern winters, so it is highly migratory, wintering in Mexico and Central America. Thus its fate is also tied to the health of tropical habitats.

But there is hope. Lewis's Woodpeckers also nest along rivers in large cottonwoods, trees of little value for timber. Furthermore, many remaining tracts of old-growth ponderosas are protected on public lands, and the trees are growing larger by the minute.

Hovering with Horned Larks

A HIGH-PITCHED, TINKLING birdsong rings across an open landscape of short grasses. A male Horned Lark hovers a hundred feet in the air—wings fluttering, circling against the blue sky. The bird glides steeply, headlong toward the ground, flaring its wings at the last instant to break the dive.

Horned Larks—roughly the size of sparrows—rival meadowlarks as the most colorful birds of the North American grasslands. The male's bright-yellow face is framed by crisp black sideburns. And true to its name, the Horned Lark does have horns, of a sort. When in the mood, the male erects pointed black feathers above its eyes, giving it a devilish appearance.

Horned Larks live in prairies, fields, and tundras. Agriculture and development now intrude on many of the Horned Lark's traditional nesting areas, so this once-common bird has become one of conservation concern. Programs that replenish grasslands and set aside croplands can be a boon to this exquisite bird.

Crow Parents

ALTHOUGH THE AMERICAN CROW may seem rather blasé about pillaging another bird's nest, it regards a threat to its own young as a punishable offense. Crows are territorial, very protective of their food sources, and ferocious and fearless as parents.

Young crows fledge, or leave the nest, when they are around five or six weeks old and nearly the same size as adults. But they still can't feed or protect themselves. Fortunately, their parents look out for them for months. In fact, crows don't mate until they are at least two years old. They often stay with the family all that time, learning from the parents and even helping with next year's brood.

To protect their young, adult crows dive-bomb people, cats, and other birds or animals. They strike with their feet, whip with their wings, and peck if they get a chance. The best thing you can do when there are baby crows around is keep your distance!

Loons Go Fishing

FOR CENTURIES, HUMANS, in gathering food, have taken advantage of the swift flight, keen sight, and diving ability of birds. Think of cormorants helping fishermen in China.

But loons have turned the tables on us. Imagine this: You're fishing a small lake in the interior of Canada. Trout rise to snatch midges and mayflies. Suddenly a trout strikes your fly. Trying to keep a tight line on the hard-fighting fish, you reel in rapidly.

But just then, you're startled to see a black-and-white figure torpedo under your boat. Alerted by the sound of your reel, a loon has followed the trout in hot pursuit. If the fish is small, the loon may take it right off the end of your line. If you succeed in bringing the trout to hand, the loon will wait for your release, in the hope of making a meal of the tired fish. To feed itself, the bird has learned to take advantage of humans.

Cattle Egret—You've Got a Friend in Me

MANY BIRDS THAT FORAGE in open country benefit from association with large grazing mammals. The big mammals scare up insects as they move, making the insects more visible to the birds. Cattle Egrets are among the most obvious of those birds. These small white herons with yellow bills are so often found with large mammals that you could think of them as friends.

Cattle Egrets in their native lands in Africa feed with elephants and rhinos and Cape buffalo. But they've become widely established in the Americas, and here they associate with cattle and horses.

A cow grazing in a pasture or a buffalo moving over the African savanna kicks up one grasshopper after another, and these egrets walk right at their feet, darting out to capture each insect as it flushes. Sharp eyed as the egrets are, they have trouble seeing the well-camouflaged grasshoppers until they move. It's good to have help from a friend sometimes.

Cuckoos Eat Hairy Tent Caterpillars

A STACCATO CALL gives away a Yellow-billed Cuckoo, lurking in a tree. One of two species of cuckoos in the woodlands of North America, the Yellow-billed lives in broadleaf forests throughout the East and riparian stands in the Southwest. They were common breeding birds in the Pacific Northwest as late as the 1920s, but then they disappeared. Ornithologists still don't know why.

The Black-billed Cuckoo is a more northerly species that lives in dense woodland, even conifer forests.

Cuckoos perch quietly and scan their surroundings for food. Hairy tent caterpillars, shunned by most birds, are often on their meal tickets. So if you have an infestation of tent caterpillars, you might see one of these slender brown-and-white birds with long white-spotted tails.

The cuckoo plucks a caterpillar from its tent and manipulates it back and forth in its bill, taking off many of the bothersome hairs. But some of them remain, and cuckoo stomachs are sometimes lined with these hairs. When the hairs are dense enough to prevent digestion, the entire stomach lining is cast off and regurgitated. Nature finds surprising ways to deal with problems!

Common Nighthawk, Uncommon Sound

THE FLIGHT CALL of the Common Nighthawk vividly evokes a warm summer evening. Loping overhead on long slender wings at dusk, the nighthawk chases down aerial insects with sudden choppy shifts of direction.

Not really a hawk at all, the Common Nighthawk is closely related to the more fully nocturnal nightjars, such as the Whip-poor-will of eastern North America. Nighthawks and nightjars have short bills but very wide-opening mouths with which they seem to vacuum up their insect prey.

Common Nighthawks migrate from Brazil and other South American countries, where they winter. They arrive with remarkable precision from these monumental journeys.

Their dark bodies are robin sized, but they have much longer wings, like two dark boomerangs propelling their erratic flight. Watch for Common Nighthawks overhead just after sunset. Or better yet, listen for them.

With luck, you may witness the male's territorial display as it dives sharply toward the earth only to pull up at the last second, while the air rushes through its wing feathers, creating a startling wallop of sound.

Chasing the Roadrunner

WHAT ANIMAL IS TWO FEET LONG, runs like the wind, loves cactus, has feathers, and catches lizards, snakes, and scorpions? What if we add that it is the most famous bird of the Southwest and has had a long run as a cartoon character? The roadrunner, of course!

Bird experts know it as the Greater Roadrunner. There's a Lesser Roadrunner in southern Mexico.

Its true voice sounds rather like a lonely puppy. The soft cooing voice hints at its connections to other birds: scientists group roadrunners with the cuckoos. The Greater Roadrunner is a common species in the desert and brush country of the Southwest, but its full range reaches from California to Western Louisiana.

For example, driving near Tucson, you might spot a Greater Roadrunner along the roadside, standing atop a boulder, eyeing you carefully. As you slow down, it raises and then lowers its crest, showing off the blue skin behind its eye. The tail levers to a high angle, then slowly pivots downward. The roadrunner is poised, ready to sprint. Ready to outrun you—or that coyote. Again.

The Bubbly Bobolink

WASHINGTON IRVING CALLED the Bobolink "the happiest bird of our spring" and added that "his life seems all song and sunshine." Emily Dickinson called the Bobolink "the rowdy of the meadow" for its bubbly, jangling song.

Bobolinks return to North America from the tropics each spring, having completed one of the longest migrations of any songbird in the Americas: roughly six thousand miles. Bobolinks fly all the way from northern Argentina to the northern United States and Canada. They cross all sorts of hazardous terrain and hundreds of miles of open water.

How do they accomplish this prodigious feat?

Bobolinks, like many birds, rely on cues from the stars and sun and from landmarks on the earth to guide them. But they also have an ace up their sleeve. Bobolinks can sense the earth's magnetic field. Their nasal tissues contain minute quantities of the mineral magnetite, providing the birds a kind of built-in compass.

Farmers who delay mowing their hayfields until midsummer or later—after the young Bobolinks have fledged—help assure the future of these amazing birds. And the Bobolinks help the farmers by eating destructive insects and the seeds of weeds.

Red-necked Phalaropes, Spinners on the Sea

RED-NECKED PHALAROPES ARE sandpipers that spend much of their life at sea. After breeding on the Arctic tundra, they migrate to the open ocean. They remain there through the winter, feeding on tiny crustaceans and other marine animals, making an amazing adaptation to a completely different environment.

Wherever you see them, these little birds will be pecking at the surface of the water. But watch for a bit, and you may see a method of feeding unique to phalaropes. They begin to twirl on the surface like little ballerinas, spinning and pecking, again and again. What are they doing?

A phalarope spins around once per second, each bird spinning only left or right. As it does so, it forces water away from itself on the surface, causing an upward flow from as deep as a foot below or more. With this flow, of course, come the tiny animals on which it feeds. Furthermore, as it opens its bill, it creates still another water current that carries prey into its throat.

One of the rewards of observing birds closely is that you see the fascinating strategies they use to survive and thrive.

Mississippi Kite

THE MISSISSIPPI KITE is one of America's most elegant raptors, with long, pointed wings and buoyant flight. These dove-gray birds spend the summer hunting over plains and woodlands in the southern United States. They often nest colonially—unusual for hawks—with a half dozen pairs in sight of one another in a grove of tall trees. By nesting in groups, they can work together to mob an approaching predator.

Medium and large insects dominate the kites' diet. During the breeding season, they seek varied prey from the treetops to the ground and even over water.

But in migration, they become more focused. By late August, the birds come together in flocks and start down the east side of Mexico, joining with tens of thousands of other migrants in the famous River of Raptors. But not only raptors. Green darners, big blue-and-green dragonflies, emerge from wetlands all over eastern North America and also head south, to breed. On their trail are the Mississippi Kites, dining on the wing, sustained by the insects that are their traveling companions.

Sparrows Kick, Robins Pick

SPARROWS KICK. ROBINS PICK. These backyard birds have different, highly evolved strategies for finding food.

Watch a White-crowned Sparrow as it forages on the leaf-covered ground. With feet held firmly side by side, it hops forward. Just as it lands, it quickly scratches backward, over-turning leaves or soil. It often does this twice in rapid succession, in a behavior so distinctive of sparrows that it has a special name: the "double-scratch." With eyes and beak trained on the ground, the sparrow is ready to snatch up any newly exposed insects or grubs or seeds.

A robin forages nearby, also atop the leaf litter. It's clearly not in on the sparrow's game, though. It doesn't double-scratch or even single-scratch. Instead, it methodically picks up or brushes aside leaf after leaf with its bill, in search of prey.

Quite a few kinds of sparrows double-scratch, so it seems to be a mark of specialists in ground feeding, often amid dense cover. Robins sometimes forage in the leaf litter, but they also seek out open, grassy areas to pluck worms from the ground, or fly up into trees in search of fruit.

So thanks to evolutionary variation, the sparrows kick, and the robins pick.

Bald Eagle, National Symbol

LOOK HIGH INTO the top branches of a tall tree, and you may see a Bald Eagle, the official bird of the United States of America.

Sitting about three feet tall, this majestic bird has a wingspan of more than six feet. Stretch your arms as far as you can, and imagine a bird whose reach is even greater.

When you see a mature Bald Eagle, you'll see a snowy-white head and tail and a dark-brown body. Look closer and you'll see lemon-yellow eyes and a powerful set of legs and feet. If you see a mottled brown bird of a similar size and shape, it's probably an immature Bald Eagle. Young eagles take up to four years to completely mature before they display majestic brown-and-white plumage. John James Audubon thought the young Bald Eagle was a new species.

Even with a call that sounds like a rusty gate, the Bald Eagle is lord of the landscape. For another look at those massive wings, take an old quarter out of your pocket. It's easy to see how the Bald Eagle earned its place as our national symbol.

The Golden One

WITH ITS IMMENSE hooked beak, striking white head, and imperious pale eyes, the Bald Eagle holds sway throughout American life. It stands proud as our national bird, spreads its wings on our national emblem, and serves as mascot of countless sports teams.

So prominent is this iconic bird in our culture that we sometimes overlook an important fact. It shares the continent with a second, equally majestic eagle: the Golden Eagle. The Golden, with a nearly seven-foot wingspan, matches the Bald Eagle in size. But its head and neck are a lustrous golden brown, the source of its name.

The two birds fill contrasting niches. Bald Eagles, which are found over much of the continent, inhabit the water's edge and prey on fish and waterbirds. Golden Eagles are birds of the West. They prefer mountain canyons and grasslands—even the Arctic tundra—where they hunt mammals, especially rabbits.

And while Bald Eagles are confined to North America, Golden Eagles are native to Europe and Asia as well. Long before the Bald Eagle adorned envelopes at the post office, the Golden Eagle flew the cosmos as personal messenger to Zeus, the ancient Greek overlord.

Gray Jay, Picnic Bird

IMAGINE VISITING MOUNT RAINIER National Park on a sunny summer day. Or Yellowstone, or Mount Katahdin in Maine. You spread out sandwiches and chips on a picnic table and turn to grab a cold drink from the cooler, when an uninvited guest arrives—a Gray Jay.

Often called the Camp Robber or Whiskey Jack, the mountain-dwelling Gray Jay seems to crash a picnic even faster than hungry ants. The fluffy, long-tailed jay is sooty gray with a white collar and forehead. And it is bold! It first hops around in a nearby tree, and then with soft, soundless flight, it drops into the middle of your camp.

The robber escapes with edible bits, which it stores by fastening them to trees with its sticky saliva. The Gray Jay breeds across northern Canada and into Alaska, reclaiming its stored food in cold, snowy, seemingly foodless conditions.

As for the nickname Whiskey Jack? That's how European settlers interpreted the Native American name for the bird. From that, they created the nickname "Whiskey John," then shortened "John" to "Jack."

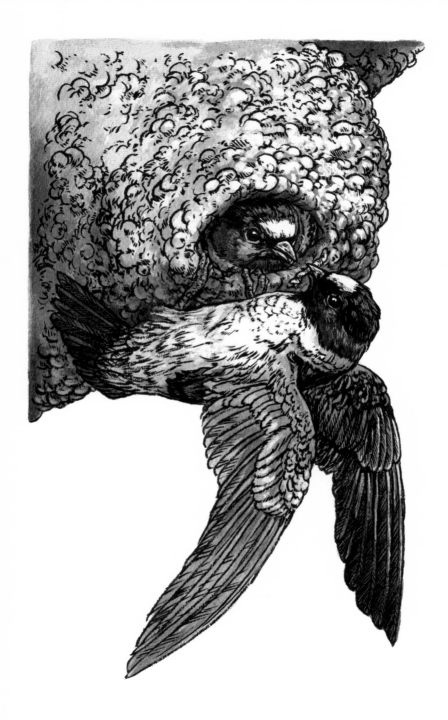

Many, Many Cliff Swallows

THE AUTHOR WILLIAM L. DAWSON wrote, "Doubtless the Lord must love the Cliff Swallows . . . else he would not have made so many of them."

When Cliff Swallows return from wintering in South America, they gather in nesting colonies. A single colony in the West may contain up to 3,700 nests. In the East, colonies are generally a bit smaller. Look for swarms of these swallows under bridges, on cliffs, under the eaves of a barns, or even on the side of a house.

They construct their gourd-shaped nests out of mud, side by side and all jumbled together. One parent usually guards the nest, often peeking out of the round opening, showing its creamy-white forehead patch.

Cliff Swallows consume hordes of flying insects. These birds have only five different calls, but one—a unique "squeak call"— tells others that they've found food. They seem to decode all this squeaking, rattling, and creaking. So when one bird finds a swarm of insects, it spreads the word to its neighbors, which is perhaps part of the reason these birds thrive in large colonies.

Outrageous Legs

VISIT A SHALLOW WETLAND in summer, and you may be dive-bombed by a slender black-and-white shorebird with outrageous red legs. The appropriately named Black-necked Stilt has the longest legs relative to its size of any North American bird. It uses those legs for wading as it picks tiny insects and crustaceans from the surface of the water with its long, slender bill.

If the stilt continues to pester you, you must be near its nest. These birds signal the approach of any potential predator. They leap into the air and call with an intensity and volume all out of proportion to their delicate appearance. The persistent calling signals that the predator has been seen and often sends it on its way. Thus, the stilt's noise and activity benefit all the birds in the vicinity.

Because of this, Black-necked Stilts are called sentinel birds. When avocets, which breed in the same habitats, add their voices to the clamor, you can understand why no sensible predator would stick around.

Birds of shallow wetlands, stilts are very sensitive to drought, which has increased with global climate change. But they readily move to new breeding areas, responding quickly when new wetlands are created.

Burrowing Belted Kingfisher

THERE'S NO OTHER SOUND along a stream or waterway quite like the reverberating metallic call of a Belted Kingfisher.

As the showy crested kingfisher flies overhead, strong staccato wing beats and white wing patches flash a Morse-code pattern. The bird's power is in its large head and sharp bill. The king of fishers hovers over water, then dives headfirst to catch its prey in its bill. Emerging from the water, the bird flies back to a perch.

There it juggles the meal—usually a fish, frog, or crawdad—into position and gulps it down.

In spring and summer, the best places to see Belted Kingfishers are along sandy banks, where they are busy at their nesting burrows. These stocky, short-legged birds use their front claws—with two forward-pointing toes fused together for added strength—and their strong bills to dig nesting holes. The holes typically reach three to six feet into the sandy bank, but some nesting holes can extend fifteen feet.

When not perching, fishing, or building a nesting burrow, the Belted Kingfisher dashes through the air, warning intruders with its rapid-fire call.

Barn Swallow, Natural Pest Control

HAS A BARN SWALLOW started slapping mud on a wall of your house in preparation for making a nest? Are you dreading the cleanup duties that will follow?

Over the years, Barn Swallows have adapted to nesting near people, and they often build their mud nests in barns or garages, on protected ledges. They seem to particularly favor ledges right above a front door. The welcome mat below becomes a pile of unwanted calling cards.

But a Barn Swallow nest above the door is also a sign of good luck. How could that be? Simple. Barn Swallows love the insects that we humans consider pesky, especially mosquitoes, gnats, and flying termites. A single Barn Swallow can consume 60 insects per hour or a whopping 850 per day. That's 25,000 fewer insects per month that might have joined your summer barbecue. Considering the hundreds of thousands of Barn Swallows all over the country, that's roughly a bazillion bugs that aren't bothering us humans. Maybe now you'll consider the chatter of the Barn Swallow to be a pleasing sound.

The Barred Owl Calls

"WHO COOKS FOR YOU? WHO COOKS FOR YOU ALL?" Both male and female Barred Owls make this signature nine-note hoot. These large gray-brown owls are very territorial, and they do not migrate, so you might hear the same birds calling, year after year.

Let's follow a young male Barred Owl through the seasons.

Throughout the late summer and fall, into winter, we hear only his solitary two-note hoots. If he had attracted a mate, there would have been a duet, a caterwauling courtship that some call the "monkey calls."

One day in April, crows create a ruckus, dive-bombing something in a tall tree—could it be our young male, trying to sleep? In May and June, he continues to hoot, though less frequently. Now, in late summer, the breeding season has passed.

What is this owl's story? Could this Barred Owl be what some scientists call a "nonbreeding floater"? Is his patch of woods just too small to host a pair of owls year-round?

Olive-sided Flycatcher: "Quick, Three Beers"

WHAT A COMFORT it would be to legions of birders if every birdsong were as easy to recognize—and remember—as that of the Olive-sided Flycatcher.

Take a walk in the mountains of the North or the West in summer, and you're likely to hear the Olive-sided Flycatcher's blithely whistled three-note song. Bird identification guides have tried to capture its pattern and quality with such catchphrases as "Quick, three beers" or "What peeves you?"

The bird's behavior also makes it easy to get to know. It perches conspicuously, bolt upright, high in the tops of dead trees. Then it sallies out to snatch flying insects. The Olive-sided Flycatcher is gray, with a peaked crown and a dark vest, and it's about eight inches long. Although it favors the edges of mountain forests, this migratory flycatcher also nests in small numbers in greenbelts and parks.

It was once a common breeder in western forests, but the bird's numbers have declined in recent decades. The reasons are unclear, but loss of trees where it winters, some four thousand miles away in South America, may be a leading cause.

Do you drink coffee? You can help Olive-sided Flycatchers when you choose to drink shade-grown beans.

How Birds Drink

THE DOG DAYS of August bring hot, sultry weather to much of North America. Just step outside, and you're already looking for a cold drink.

Birds need liquids too. Some birds can go a long time without drinking, even in sweltering habitats. They metabolize water from foods, even dry foods such as seeds, and reabsorb fluids internally rather than excreting them.

Other birds eagerly seek out water on hot days. Songbirds, like robins, find water at a stream or birdbath. A robin takes a mouthful of water, then tips its head way back to send the water down its gullet. Pigeons drink differently. They're among the few birds that can suck in water with their heads down.

Swallows and swifts drink with enviable grace. Gliding low across a pond, a swallow tilts its wings upward, lowers its head to the water's surface, and skims a beakful of water on the wing. And it makes it look so easy.

Keep your birdbath full, yes, and keep it clean, or the birds could be picking up a disease with that mouthful of water.

Great Blue Heron,
Alone Again

A PREHISTORIC-SOUNDING CALL is coming from a Great Blue Heron. This tall, stately bird is commonly seen standing alone on beaches, in marshes, on docks and pilings, and even on tree branches. Watching. Waiting.

In the spring, herons form groups for nesting, constructing their spartan stick nests in adjoining trees. Several nests may be crammed into one tree, and a colony can contain as many as sixty nests, creating quite a frenzy! Nesting in large colonies helps protect the young from predators.

But by late summer, the adults and gangly young have left the nests to take up solitary lives along beaches, marshes, lake edges, and rivers. After all the togetherness of the nesting colonies, the herons spend the off-season by themselves, a pattern that is the reverse of many other species. During fall and winter, they defend the areas where they feed as adamantly as other birds defend their nesting territories in spring. The herons challenge and scare away intruders, including other Great Blue Herons, by sounding a call. Alone again.

Autumnal Equinox

THE AUTUMNAL EQUINOX: midpoint between June's longest day and December's shortest day. We may hardly notice it, but ancient cultures closely watched the changes in the sun's daily patterns.

One legend from the Andes of South America explained the sun's movement across the sky this way: only the giant Andean Condor, with its ten-foot wingspan, had the strength to lift the sun each morning and pull it back down each evening. This work allowed the condor to communicate with the sun god and gave the condor healing properties. Ingesting the dried heart of a condor, it was believed, could cure epilepsy and heart disease, and eating ground condor bones would alleviate rheumatism.

We now know that the Andean Condor is the largest flying bird in the Western Hemisphere, and possibly the world. Plumed in black, with white wing patches, condors travel up to two hundred miles a day, foraging for dead or dying animals. These huge birds have been known to drag carcasses weighing forty-four pounds.

That's quite a cargo for the thirty-pound Andean Condor. But it's nothing compared to the task of dragging the sun up each morning and back down each evening.

The Oystercatcher's World

STAND ON A ROCKY SHORELINE on the Pacific Coast, and you might just hear the piping call of a Black Oystercatcher. It's a stocky black bird with bright-red eyes and a stout orange-red bill perfectly suited for jabbing limpets and mussels.

A strong ebb tide is flowing, creating whirlpools and tugging at the kelp. On nearby rocks, harbor seals, looking like huge taut sausages, are resting.

The oystercatcher is completely dependent on this marine shoreline for nesting and food, even in winter, when waves hit the rocks with awesome force. Yet what seems like an inhospitable environment to us offers some advantages to the oystercatcher.

For one, when the monogamous Black Oystercatcher nests on ledges just offshore, its eggs and young suffer far less predation by mammals. For another, wave-splashed mussels, the bird's chief food, open more often, making them easier to attack and eat. And contrary to their name, oystercatchers rarely eat oysters.

Common Murres, Nature's Laugh Track

THE SOUND OF RAUCOUS LAUGHTER, a little deranged, rings out above the crash of ocean waves. The voices belong to birds, a nesting colony of Common Murres standing on narrow ledges high on the steep face of a sea cliff. Precarious as their nest site is, Common Murres nest by the thousands along the Pacific Coast, perhaps by the millions north along the Bering Sea.

The chocolate-brown murres stand nearly a foot and a half tall, on legs set far back on their bodies. Add to this their sharply pointed bills, and murres look much like the northern equivalent of the penguins of the Southern Hemisphere.

The female murre lays a single large egg. It is pointed at one end and blunt at the other, so it spins on the ledge rather than tumbling into the sea below.

The Common Murre's guttural call carries well over the roar of the waves, a natural laugh track far richer than human laughter canned for a sitcom.

Swifts Roost by the Thousands

JUST WHAT IS IT that could bring crowds of people out after sunset on a September evening to stare at . . . a chimney?

Scores—perhaps hundreds—of small dark birds are gathering. They whirl by, then form a funnel-shaped cloud above the chimney. Now they begin to descend, first one, then a few more, then dozens, then hundreds, swirling right down into the chimney. Each bird goes in with its wings held high, as if parachuting, dropping inside to catch onto the rough interior, where it will hang until morning.

A flock of Chimney Swifts has just entered its communal roost site for the night. These birds spend much of the year far to the south, in the Amazon basin of Peru. But in the spring, they head north, east of the Rockies, to nest. West of the Rockies, Vaux's Swifts perform the same autumn ritual before they head south to Central America.

The number of Chimney Swifts has dropped in recent years, in part because good old-fashioned chimneys are harder to find. You can help by altering an existing chimney or providing a roosting tower to make swifts feel more at home.

Why Geese Fly in V-Formation

AMONG THE MOST EVOCATIVE sounds of early autumn are the voices of migratory geese flying high overhead. Canada Geese are migrating after nesting in Canada and Alaska.

But what about that V-formation angling outward like a ship's wake through the sky? This phenomenon—a kind of synchronized, aerial tailgating—marks the flight of flocks of larger birds, like geese or pelicans, but isn't seen in smaller birds, like robins or sandpipers.

Most observers believe there is a straightforward reason for the birds to fly in a V. Each bird behind the leader is taking advantage of the lift of a corkscrew of air coming off the wingtips of the bird in front. This corkscrew updraft is called a "tip vortex." Such efficiency enables the geese to save considerable energy during long flights.

The V-formation may also enhance birds' ability to see and hear each other, thus preventing midair collisions. So migrating birds that fly in a V combine the benefits of aerial updrafts and communication.

Small birds probably do not create enough of an updraft to help others in the flock, so they don't fly in V-formation.

Why Is Bird Poop White?

BIRDS BRIGHTEN OUR LIVES. We find joy in their songs, inspiration in their soaring flight. They connect us with nature.

But sometimes birds connect us a bit too directly with nature.

Park under the wrong tree—one where a flock of starlings or grackles comes to roost—and nature may be painted in white on your car so thickly that it takes a trip or two through the car wash just to see through the windshield again.

Aside from helping you decide where not to park next time, this messy event raises a scientific question: Why is most of the bird poop we see white? The answer lies in the fact that birds, unlike mammals, don't produce urine. Instead they excrete nitrogenous wastes in the form of uric acid, which emerges as a white paste. And uric acid doesn't dissolve in water easily. Hence its ability to stick to your windshield like blobs of white plaster.

It appears that drivers of some cars might be asking for trouble. A study in England found that red cars are most likely to be the target of bird droppings, followed by blue and black. Green was the least likely. So be careful where you park. And give that red Mustang a wide berth.

The Spectacular and Endangered California Condor

IT'S A LOVELY DAY along the California coast, near Big Sur. A steady, cooling breeze from the ocean pushes a strong updraft along the seaside cliffs. Soaring above is one of North America's most spectacular birds—and one of its most endangered—the California Condor.

California Condors are the largest soaring birds in North America, with a wingspan of over nine feet. During the days of mammoths and saber-toothed cats, they thrived over much of the continent. Two hundred years ago, condors were found from California to southern British Columbia.

But by 1987, there were only twenty-seven California Condors left, and these were held in captivity, to foster the species' return to the wild. Today, there are nearly five hundred living in the wild or in captivity.

Yet the wild population is not self-sustaining. Unlike many species, the condor's main survival problem is not habitat loss—it's high mortality due to lead poisoning. Condors eat animal carcasses, which often contain lead from hunters' bullets. But a state law passed in California in 2013 aims to eliminate the use of lead completely by 2019. That's a change that could enable condors to once again thrive and soar in the Golden State and beyond.

The Lowly Starling

MUCH MALIGNED AS a pest and cursed by many as an invasive species, the European Starling has had many fans too. Eugene Schieffelin thought enough of the starling—or of Shakespeare—to introduce about fifty pairs into the United States in the 1890s. Schieffelin attempted to bring all the birds mentioned in Shakespeare's plays into this country.

Rachel Carson, author of *Silent Spring,* said of the starling, "In spite of his remarkable success as a pioneer, the starling probably has fewer friends than almost any other creature that wears feathers." But she also noted that he carries "more than one hundred loads of destructive insects per day to his screaming offspring."

No less a figure than Wolfgang Amadeus Mozart kept a pet starling. The story goes that while Mozart was rehearsing his Piano Concerto no. 17 in G Major, the bird began whistling along. The composer liked the bird's contribution so much that he actually wrote it into the concerto's grace notes. And when Mozart's beloved starling died, he wrote a poem about it.

Eastern Whip-poor-will—
Bird of the Night Side
of the Woods

IN SEPTEMBER 1851, Henry David Thoreau wrote, "The Whip-poor-wills now begin to sing in earnest about half an hour before sunrise, as if making haste to improve the short time that is left them. . . . They sing for several hours in the early part of the night . . . then sing again just before sunrise."

Clearly and continuously, the bird announces its name. From summer to early fall, Eastern Whip-poor-wills breed in the woodlands of eastern North America. Their camouflaged plumage blends seamlessly with dead leaves on the forest floor. At dawn and dusk and all through moonlit nights, whip-poor-wills sally out from tree branches to hawk flying insects.

Woodland habitat has greatly diminished for Eastern Whip-poor-wills as forests have become more fragmented. The National Audubon Society lists them among the top twenty common birds in decline. Protecting and restoring large expanses of forest are crucial for many forest species, including the whip-poor-will.

It remains, as Thoreau described, "a bird . . . of the night side of the woods . . . where you may hear the whip-poor-will in your dreams."

The Eyes of an Owl

AN OWL'S GAZE is uniquely penetrating. Peer into an owl's face—there is something almost human about its large, forward-facing eyes.

Just how big are those eyes? They are astonishingly large in proportion to the size of the owl's head. A Great Gray Owl, which stands two feet tall and weighs two and a half pounds, has eyes larger than those of most humans!

And while an owl's eyes may look human, their capabilities are superhuman. Enormous eyes help owls to see in near darkness. An owl's retinal anatomy is similar to that of cats, which rival owls in seeing in dim light.

Owls see well in daylight too, but their color vision is probably very limited. And the evolution of such large eyes has required a behavioral compromise: an owl's eyes are fixed in their sockets, so the bird must rotate its neck to look around.

One ornithologist, Dr. Paul A. Johnsgard, described owls' heads as "little more than brains with raptorial beaks and the largest possible eyes and ears attached."

Freeway Hawks

DRIVING THE FREEWAY, perhaps just inching along in traffic, you happen to glance up at an overhead light post where a large hawk sits in plain view. It is brown, somewhat mottled; a small head and short tail make it appear football shaped. It's a Red-tailed Hawk.

During winter, many Red-tailed Hawks move south, joining year-round resident pairs, to feed on mice, voles, and other small mammals. The freeway's wide center medians and mowed shoulders offer a mini-habitat of open grassland where Red-tailed Hawks watch for prey. And the light posts, telephone poles, and nearby trees offer excellent viewing perches.

The bird's red tail may be hard to see, since folded wings often cover it. If your view is of the bird's front, watch for a dark bellyband across the lower part of its pale chest. If your view is of its back, try to observe a white spotted *V* in the center of the back. You'll see the red tail when it flies. Perhaps a bit of freeway birdwatching may ease the frustration of slow traffic, so watch for this bulky football of a hawk. Once Red-tails find a successful hunting area, they return often.

The Crows' Night Roost

CROWS STREAM BY overhead in the late afternoon—rivers of crows. These are American Crows with a purpose. They're headed to their night roost, a giant avian slumber party.

Gathering in a park or woodland, they land in a tree, then scuffle and shuffle and squawk, filtering down through the branches. Birds arriving late force the early birds lower into the trees. Crow expert Bil Gilbert believed that the roost provides warmth, protection from predators, knowledge about food sources, and a chance to locate a mate.

Immature crows may spend the night in the roost year-round, but adults of breeding age generally use the roost only during the nonbreeding seasons.

And just how many crows are there in a roost? It depends, but one long-time roost in Danville, Illinois, boasts more than a hundred thousand birds. Not that the folks of Danville are especially happy about that. Imagine the ruckus when the first few thousand crows leave in the morning, about an hour before sunrise.

Follow crows to their roost some autumn evening, if you can, and watch these avian acrobats wheel in. Hitchcock's movie *The Birds* might come to mind. And if you go, a word of warning: you'd better take an umbrella.

Chorus Line in the Sky

WHAT IS THAT cloud low in the autumn sky, shape-shifting as you watch from a beach or mudflat and suddenly flashing from dark to light? It's a cloud of small sandpipers called Dunlins. When threatened by a falcon, for instance, Dunlins take to the air, flying so close together that it's hard for a predator to capture one. The Dunlins' synchronous twisting and turning is a marvel of aerial acrobatics, with the birds alternately flashing brown backs and white bellies. The speed of change is breathtaking, with hundreds of birds turning simultaneously.

Biologist Wayne Potts, curious about the lack of midair collisions (and speculating about extrasensory communication), filmed a few of these flocks. He found that a bird at one edge turns toward the middle and a wave sweeps across the entire flock in less than a second. Like a member of a chorus line, each bird sees the movement beginning to happen and makes the appropriate response.

Do Canada Geese Migrate?

THE CALLS OF CANADA GEESE flying high overhead in a long, gangly V-formation—one of our most familiar wild sounds. And it's one of our most enduring emblems of the change of seasons.

October is the peak month in the southward migration of Canada Geese, which breed in summer in Canada and Alaska. "But," you may ask, "aren't there Canada Geese around all through the year, on park lawns and golf courses? Where do these geese fit into the picture?"

It's complicated. The birds we think of as Canada Geese—brown geese with a white chinstrap marking—actually comprise a whole range of geographic populations. Some are larger, some smaller, and most subgroups have distinct breeding ranges north of the US border. However, some Canada Geese are now largely nonmigratory, much to the chagrin of golfers and others. Many of the geese that now stay year-round are the descendants of birds introduced by game-management authorities in an effort to revive some of the original wild populations that had been decimated before the 1900s.

So while some Canada Geese are migratory, flying thousands of miles each year between nesting and wintering sites, others are happy to stick around. We humans have made them an offer they can't refuse: acres and acres of delectable grass on lawns, parks, and golf courses.

Ring-necked Pheasants in the Wild

THE RING-NECKED PHEASANT is likely the best-known bird in North America that isn't actually native to the continent. Indigenous to east and central Asia, Ring-necked Pheasants were brought in from China in 1881 to foster a viable pheasant population in Oregon. The birds spread throughout the Northwest, and some of them were introduced to the Midwest and other parts of the country.

Ring-necked Pheasants owe much of their expansion across the continent to their popularity as game birds. Hunters and

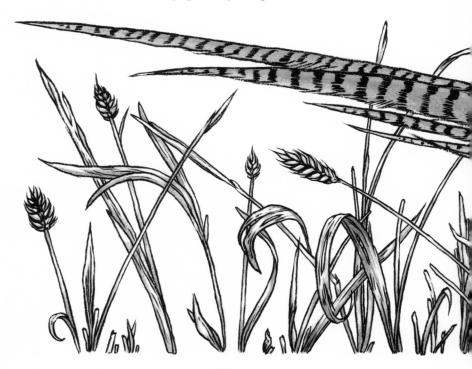

birders alike admire the cock pheasant's spectacular, ornate feathering. And for many years, pheasants thrived in the country's rural landscapes, where small farms offered hayfields and fallow acres, and where hedgerows and stands of trees provided cover for the birds.

Today, though, industrial farming practices leave less and less for pheasants. Hedgerows are disappearing, weedy cover is burned or sprayed with weed killer, pheasant nests succumb to more frequent hay mowing, and livestock overgraze grasslands.

But there is hope for wild pheasants: in some areas of the country, wildlife agencies are working with private landowners to help create favorable habitats, giving the birds the cover they need for feeding, nesting, and roosting through the seasons.

"Fly Me to the Moon," the Story of a Red Knot

EVER THOUGHT OF flying to the moon? You'd need to buckle up for a flight of 239,000 miles. That's roughly the same as circling the Earth ten times.

But you still wouldn't have flown as far as a Red Knot named B95. A tag was first placed on this male sandpiper's leg in 1995. Red Knots migrate about sixteen thousand miles round-trip each year. They nest above the Arctic Circle and winter near the tip of South America. That means B95's cumulative migration flights would have carried him to the moon—and he'd already be on his way back.

In spite of the birds' astonishing abilities, Red Knot populations have declined severely in recent decades. The migrating birds rely on critical resting and feeding areas such as Delaware Bay. In South America, conservation groups, including Manomet and the international organization Rare, are helping protect at least three crucial wintering sites in Argentina.

Red Knots and other long-distance travelers deserve—and depend upon—healthy coastal ecosystems throughout the Western Hemisphere.

Everybody Knows a Mallard

A BIRD IS MAKING a familiar quacking sound. It's our most recognizable duck, the Mallard. But did you know that only the female Mallard *quacks*?

In its breeding plumage, the male Mallard is an avian dandy. It sports a metallic-green head, lemon-yellow bill, narrow white collar, and chestnut breast. Brilliant blue-violet feathers flash midway down its wings. In case that isn't enough to lure female Mallards, a charming curl adorns the male's central tail feathers, unlike any other bird in North America. Female Mallards, on the other hand, are plumed in subdued mottled browns.

The male's primary goal is to attract a mate and defend the breeding territory. The female's is to blend in with the natural surroundings while incubating the eggs and caring for the young.

Fairly soon after the breeding season—say, June or July—watch for the males to become quite drab. Mallards molt at this time—their old feathers come out, and new ones will begin to grow in.

Yet despite any outward changes in plumage, the female's ability to quack loudly never diminishes during the year.

Ducks: Diving and Dabbling

AUTUMN BRINGS MILLIONS of ducks flying south after they've nested in the north. In most parts of North America, fall migration brings the greatest diversity of ducks we'll see all year. Goldeneyes, scaup, wigeons, and other species join familiar year-round ducks such as Mallards.

Take a close look at autumn's ducks as they forage on the water. Some dabble, while others dive.

Dabbling ducks, such as wigeons, feed by dipping their bills just below the surface of the water or dunking headfirst, so all you see are their tails pointing skyward. They strain bits of vegetation and small invertebrates with their flattened bills.

Diving ducks, including scaup and mergansers, forage while swimming underwater, using their feet or wings for propulsion. Divers with narrow, pointed bills snatch fish, while those with flatter bills, like Common Goldeneyes, search along the bottom for invertebrates such as small clams.

When you stop by a lake or a saltwater beach this fall, keep an eye out for dabblers and divers. And take your time, because the divers may pop into view only when they need to catch a breath of air.

How Brown Pelicans Dive

IMAGINE A LINE OF Brown Pelicans flying just above the breaking surf of the coast. Perhaps you've watched—and heard—these large, long-billed birds fishing. They circle high, then dive headfirst, plunging underwater to catch fish.

But doesn't that hurt? Anyone who has done a belly flop off a diving board knows the powerful force of hitting the water. Several adaptations protect Brown Pelicans as they dive, sometimes from as high as sixty feet. Air sacs beneath the skin on their breasts act like cushions. Also, while diving, a pelican rotates its body ever so slightly to the left. This rotation helps avoid injury to the esophagus and trachea, which are located on the right side of the bird's neck. Pelicans have also learned that a steep dive angle—between sixty and ninety degrees—reduces aiming errors caused by water surface refraction. We know that pelicans learn this behavior over time, because adults are better marksmen than young birds are.

Upon impact, the Brown Pelican opens its bill and expands its pouch, trapping small fish inside. Then the bird pops to the surface, spills out the water, and gulps down dinner.

Carrier Pigeons Go to War

IN TODAY'S WORLD of texting and Skyping, it's amazing to think that not long ago, the most reliable means of long-distance communication was provided by birds. Those birds were carrier pigeons—specially trained members of the same species as our familiar city Rock Pigeons.

The time of their utmost value was World War I. Although messages could be sent over field phones, conditions of war—particularly at the front, where battles raged—often made laying phone wires impossible. Pigeons were crucial in relaying messages from the front to positions behind the lines. This was done by enclosing a note in a tiny canister attached to the bird's leg.

The most renowned carrier pigeon was Cher Ami—or Dear Friend—flown by the United States Army Signal Corps during the Battle of Verdun in France. The message Cher Ami carried on October 4, 1918, was vital in saving hundreds of American soldiers of the now-famed "Lost Battalion" of the Seventy-Seventh Infantry. Cher Ami delivered the message despite being badly wounded, losing an eye and a leg to German gunfire. The esteemed pigeon later received the French Croix de Guerre, one of the country's greatest honors.

Reddish Egret, Lagoon Dancer

ON THE GULF of Mexico, a long, low sandbar marks the entrance to a protected expanse of water—a lagoon. Small fish dart across the lagoon, riffling the ankle-deep water. A Reddish Egret waits, watching alertly.

The Reddish Egret, a particularly glamorous heron with a long neck, is named for its ruffled neck plumes, which gleam like burnished copper. The egret stands nearly three feet tall, on lanky cobalt-blue legs. Its bill, a long pink dagger, is tipped in black.

Exquisite, yes. But Reddish Egrets are best known for their startling antics in capturing fish. When fishing, the egret sprints across the lagoon, weaving left and right, simultaneously flicking its broad wings in and out while stabbing into the water with its bill. Fish startled at the egret's crazed movements become targets of that pink dagger.

This is just one of the Reddish Egret's several fishing tactics. At times, the bird will raise its wings forward over its head, creating a shadow on the water. It then freezes in this position for minutes. Fish swim in, attracted by a patch of shade, and . . . well, you know the rest.

A Blizzard of Snow Geese

A WILD SOUND—some liken it to the baying of hounds—pours from the sky each autumn along all four North American flyways. Millions of Snow Geese are returning from their Arctic breeding grounds, thousands of geese in any one flock.

Snow Geese fly high, a cloud of snowflakes against the blue sky, periodically stopping over en masse at staging points across the continent. They are bound for traditional wintering areas along the South Atlantic and Gulf Coasts, and in the western states and Mexico.

Imagine a visit to one of their wintering sites, whether it be the rice fields of Southern Louisiana, the Skagit River Delta in Washington State, or New Mexico's Bosque del Apache preserve. As you look across a broad expanse of browns and greens, a pattern of dark soil interspersed with planted fields, your eyes come to rest on one field that appears to be covered in snow. A closer look reveals ten thousand or more white-feathered Snow Geese blanketing the field in one immense flock.

And listen when a Bald Eagle flies over and the multitudes take flight in a spectacular avian blizzard, their joined voices all but deafening.

Northern Cardinal,
Star of Holiday Cards
and Team Jerseys

EVEN WITHOUT TAKING a poll, is there any doubt about the identity of America's best-known red bird? Surely it's the cardinal—or, as you'll find it called in a bird book, the Northern Cardinal.

The cardinal's crested scarlet image adorns Christmas cards, bags of birdseed, and any number of sports teams' jerseys. It is simply—and being red doesn't hurt here—one of our best-known backyard birds.

So would it surprise you to learn that cardinals are missing from backyards in nearly half of the United States? It's the half west of the Rockies. Or that only about half of all cardinals are red? Females are olive brown, with a few red highlights.

It's also true that the cardinal seen on so many bird feeders takes its name from the cardinals found in the Vatican, whose hats and robes are red.

And among the cardinal's near relatives—the cardinal on the bird feeder, that is—two are also very red birds: the Summer Tanager and the Scarlet Tanager. But despite their beauty, tanagers are unlikely to unseat the cardinal as our best-known red bird.

Acknowledgments

BIRDNOTE WOULD LIKE TO THANK the following for their contributions to *BirdNote* and to this book: *BirdNote* founder, executive producer emeritus, and writer Chris Peterson; John Fitzpatrick, Matthew Young, and The Macaulay Library at the Cornell Lab of Ornithology for providing most of the sounds heard in *BirdNote* shows; the board, staff, and production team at *BirdNote*, past and present; Lauri Adams and Mark Wittow for pro bono legal counsel; composer Nancy Rumbel and producer John Kessler for creating *BirdNote*'s distinctive theme music; volunteer researcher Beth Cordova; the volunteers, listeners, and fans who contribute ideas, photographs, blogs, sounds, and videos to *BirdNote*'s stories and website; KNKX—the radio station that helped *BirdNote* take to the airwaves; *BirdNote*'s partners, including National Audubon, American Bird Conservancy, Ducks Unlimited, Environment for the Americas, National Environmental Education Foundation, the Endangered Species Coalition, and Partners in Flight; and the generous individual donors, foundations, and corporate supporters that make all of *BirdNote*'s work possible.

Listen to the Stories

FOR A COMPLETE LIST of web links to the stories in this book, where you can hear the narrations and bird sounds and read the original transcripts with full credits, please visit BirdNote.org/Book.

Index

The BirdNote Team

BirdNote is written by a team of scientists and bird lovers who share a passion for science and great storytelling. Lead writer Bob Sundstrom, PhD, leads birding tours all over the world and has a special interest in birding by ear. Gordon Orians, PhD, is an ecologist whose research has emphasized birds. Biologist Dennis Paulson, PhD, has a particular interest in dragonflies and shorebirds. Gordon and Dennis also vet each story for scientific accuracy. Other accomplished writers from across the country add their historical, sociological, and literary expertise, creating stories that are joyful, inspirational, and rooted in science. These writers include Ellen Blackstone, Sallie Bodie, Frank Corrado, GrrlScientist, John Kessler, Chris Peterson, Todd Peterson, Bryan Pfeiffer, Gerrit Vyn, Frances Wood, Rick Wright, and the late Idie Ulsh. Todd Peterson, Chris Peterson, and Dominic Black edited the original stories for radio.

Editor Ellen Blackstone is a writer and associate producer for *BirdNote*. She previously edited *Earthcare Northwest*, the newsletter of Seattle Audubon. She volunteered with the Seattle Peregrine Project and was a longtime member of the American Society of Crows and Ravens.